COMPUTER RESOURCE GUIDE

PRINCIPLES OF ACCOUNTING

FOURTH EDITION

JOHN W. WANLASS, C.P.A.
De Anza College

THE DRYDEN PRESS
Harcourt Brace Jovanovich College Publishers
Fort Worth   Philadelphia   San Diego   New York   Orlando   Austin   San Antonio
Toronto   Montreal   London   Sydney   Tokyo

Address for Editorial Correspondence
The Dryden Press, 301 Commerce Street, Suite 3700, Fort Worth, TX 76102

Address for Orders
The Dryden Press, 6277 Sea Harbor Drive, Orlando, FL 32887
1-800-782-4479, or 1-800-433-0001 (in Florida)

ISBN: 0-03-097409-7

Printed in the United States of America

3 4 5 6 7 8 9 0 1 2 066 9 8 7 6 5 4 3 2 1

The Dryden Press
Harcourt Brace & Company

Preface

Tho oinglo objootivo of tho *Computer Resource Guide: Principles of Accounting*, fourth edition, is to bridge the widening gap between the methods used in accounting practice and the methods used in the accounting classroom. In accounting practice, the computer is a universal tool used by companies of any size, large or small. In the accounting classroom, students are exposed to manual accounting methods, which for the most part do not reflect current practices in the so-called real world.

The nature of that gap is changing over time. Students are better prepared to deal with computers than they were even three and four years ago. The computing environment in real-world practice has also moved forward. Two types of computer application programs are in widespread use. Procedural programs such as general ledger software and declarative programs including electronic spreadsheets are found in almost every business office. Exposure to and experience with both types of programs are required in today's complex business environment. Both are covered in this student workbook.

Although the guide is intended to be used as an integral part of the first-year accounting course, its coverage is broad enough to be used in a separate computer accounting course or as a computer introduction and review for intermediate accounting. The approach is pragmatic: Typical accounting problems are given in a form familiar to the first-year student. These problems are then organized and processed by the student using the computer as a tool.

Historically, computers have been introduced toward the end of the accounting program. However, with the advent of the small business computer, the student is faced with the opportunity and the necessity to use and understand the computer. In today's business world, computer literacy is almost mandatory. A student who feels comfortable using a computer and has a working knowledge of electronic spreadsheets, has marketable job skills that are greatly magnified.

Accounting activity can be grouped in one of two categories: activity that involves processing business transactions or activity that involves analyzing business problems. The following chart compares the methods used in the classroom with the methods used in practice, grouped by type of activity.

	Processing Transactions	**Analyzing Problems**
Classroom	Manual Accounting Cycle	Manual Spreadsheets
Practice	Computer Accounting Cycle	Electronic Spreadsheets

Because of the basic differences between the computer accounting cycle and the use of electronic spreadsheets, the guide is presented in two parts: Part One covers the accounting cycle and Part Two covers the electronic spreadsheet.

PART ONE   The Accounting Cycle - *Processing Business Transactions*

Using a flexible and easy-to-learn general ledger software program, you will design and establish a computer accounting system for a number of different companies. The software uses Visible Accounting Systems, or VAS, a software program that allows you to design a suitable chart of accounts and define the financial statement account categories for each company. Unlike existing computer practice sets, VAS is a true computer accounting system that can be used to process other transaction-based problems, not just the problems contained in this manual.

Part One consists of six chapters. *Chapter 1* provides an important overview of the difference between manual and computer accounting systems. *Chapter 2* provides operating instructions, and *Chapter 3* is a sample problem to walk the student through the system. *Chapter 4* is a detailed description of the various functions available. *Chapter 5* provides 10 practical problem applications of increasing complexity. *Chapter 6* is a two-part practice set that follows the growth of a fictional company through its first six months of operations.

At the completion of Part One, you will be prepared to set up an accounting system for any new company or convert an existing company from a manual system to a computer system.

The VAS general ledger software program gives you features that will ease the transition from manual accounting to computer accounting. Here is a partial list of features:

1. A colorful, intuitive user interface. You open an onscreen "book" to access financial records. You will be able to use most options by making a single keystroke—whether to move from one menu to the next, to select an operation, or to process the selection.

2. A stepwise approach to menu structure. You can escape out of an activity one step at a time.

3. Bottom-line menu and command bar. You always see the current menu and a list of current options at the bottom of the screen.

4. Onscreen help always available. By pressing the <F1> key at any time, you open a pop-up book of helpful advice and instructions.

5. Powerful input routines. You can add, modify, and delete transactions. You can add a transaction anywhere within the journal.

6. Fast and easy auditing routines. Simply by pressing the left and right arrow keys, you can move from a chart of accounts to the journal, to the ledger, and on to various financial statements.

7. Flexible data storage. You can choose to save data to any active drive.

8. File capacity. You can create files with up to 150 accounts in the chart of accounts and up to 250 double-entry transactions.

9. Minimal system requirements. The VAS program will run from a floppy disk or a hard disk and is not copy protected. VAS will run with only 256K RAM memory and DOS 2.1 or higher. Because you can use VAS with a single floppy disk double-sided disk drive, you can use the program with almost any IBM PC microcomputer or compatible.

PART TWO The Electronic Spreadsheet - *Analyzing Business Problems*

With <u>Lotus 1-2-3</u> software, a widely used electronic spreadsheet program, you will learn to organize and process a variety of financial and managerial accounting problems. (This commercial software is to be supplied by you or your school.) You will solve and program each problem manually using a worksheet that is provided. You will then create an electronic version of your worksheet and analyze your solutions.

Part Two consists of seven chapters. *Chapter 7* provides a short perspective of electronic spreadsheets. *Chapter 8* introduces <u>Lotus 1-2-3</u> through practice exercises covering the basic spreadsheet mechanics. *Chapter 9* is a comprehensive tutorial using two sample problems. *Chapters 10, 11, 12, and 13* are practical applications of financial and managerial problems from the first-year accounting course. In *Chapter 13* you will design, program, and use selected spreadsheets.

Because data files for both Part One and Part Two are stored on the distribution disk, it may be necessary to manage the available disk space. All <u>Lotus 1-2-3</u> files are in Release 2 format (.WK1).

At the completion of Part Two, you will be prepared to design, program, and create electronic spreadsheets covering a wide range of accounting problems. Also, and most important, you will be proficient in electronic spreadsheet skills that are readily transferable to the business world.

Appendix A provides a brief overview of the IBM PC microcomputer. Appendix B is a correlation of problems for <u>Principles of Accounting</u>, sixth edition, by Hanson, Hamre, and Walgenbach, published by Harcourt Brace Jovanovich, Inc. Because the problems selected are similar to those found in any accounting principles or financial accounting textbook, the guide can be used to support any accounting textbook.

There are special forms at the back of the guide. The forms for Part One are used to establish the accounting system for the general ledger program. The forms for Part Two provide an analysis sheet for each of the electronic spreadsheet problems. Most of the analysis sheets also include an alternate problem to be solved using your programmed worksheet.

An instructor's manual and solutions disk are available to adopters of the *Computer Resource Guide*. In addition to detailed solutions for each problem, the manual includes suggestions for use in the accounting principles course and alternative methods for managing data files created by the student. The disk contains completed files for most of the assigned material.

I hope that with a more productive view of the accounting cycle and a working knowledge of electronic spreadsheets, you will gain a deeper understanding of the principles of accounting and be better prepared to face the challenges of the business world.

John W. Wanlass

Contents

PART ONE

■

The Accounting Cycle

The Accounting Cycle

Debits = Credits

Assets = Liabilities + ?

RECORD	Journals
CLASSIFY	Ledgers
SUMMARIZE	Trial Balance
CATEGORIZE	Financial Statements
ANALYZE	Ratios, Trends

Systems in General

We are constantly exposed to various systems. The human body is a system that in turn consists of many subsystems. The judicial system comprises human thoughts and ideas. Distribution systems for transportation and communication are an integral part of our lives.

Certain attributes are common to all systems. For example, a system is made up of parts or components. The parts are related or interdependent. Components work together toward common goals. A change in one component is likely to produce changes in other components and the system as a whole. Systems are usually complex, being composed of diverse elements. Each system is likely to be part of another system, just as it is likely to be divided into many subsystems.

Business Information Systems

Business information systems are like other systems: They consist of components that work together toward a common goal. The goal of a business information system is to provide the basis for making *informed* and *effective decisions.* Let's examine how a business information system works.

Business activity is recorded in the form of contracts, memos, and other source documents. These are often referred to as **data**. (See the diagram on the next page.) Usually these data must be processed in some manner before the human mind can see meaningful relationships between individual documents. There are almost too many terms used to describe this process: associating, comparing, sorting, reducing, summarizing, grouping, classifying, and many more! For our purpose, think of data processing as data organization.

When data are processed, they are converted into **information**. The basic difference between data and information is that *data are unorganized* and *information is organized*. Information is useful for making decisions because it is organized. However, information alone does not provide the basis for decisions. Without a careful analysis of information, its value is minimal. Information when properly analyzed or interpreted can lead to **knowledge**. This is the real basis for making decisions.

In summary, a business information system organizes and analyzes the records (data) of business activity to provide a basis for making decisions.

Business Information Systems

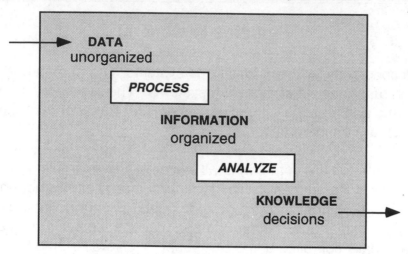

Accounting Information Systems

An accounting information system provides financial information essential to the decision-making process. As part of the overall business information system, the accounting system plays a large role in organizing raw data into a form that is manageable. The process of organizing data is a focal point in our study of the accounting cycle.

Business activity is documented in the form of *source documents,* which must be analyzed and recorded. The source document represents a *transaction* to which the business has agreed. The company is responsible for the effects of the transaction. From the company's point of view, every transaction is composed of two parts, that which is received and that which is given. In the bookkeepers' world, these translate as debits and credits.

All transactions are analyzed in terms of their effects on the major financial statements, the <u>balance sheet</u> and the <u>income statement</u>. The balance sheet is grouped by assets, liabilities, and owner equity. Within each grouping are the related <u>accounts</u>. The income statement is grouped by revenues, costs, and expenses. These groups also consist of their related accounts. Collectively, all of the accounts are referred to as the <u>chart of accounts</u>.

Transactions must be directed to their financial statement destination by a process called *account coding.* The two parts of each transaction must be coded with the appropriate account code. This must be done before transactions can be entered into a computer system.

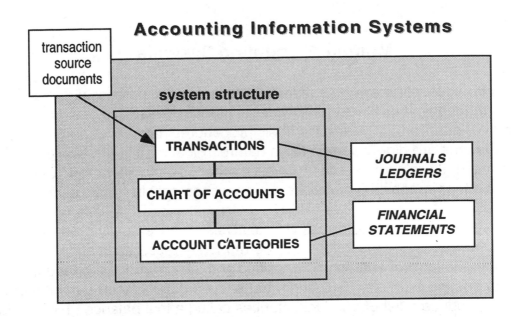

Accounting Information Systems

transaction source documents

system structure

TRANSACTIONS

CHART OF ACCOUNTS

ACCOUNT CATEGORIES

JOURNALS LEDGERS

FINANCIAL STATEMENTS

Once the system structure is defined and established, two different views of all the *transaction detail* can be obtained. They are referred to as the journals and the ledger. The only difference between them is that the journals list the transactions by *date* and the ledger lists the transactions by *account*. Transactions can be summarized and reported in the form of a trial balance and financial statements.

In summary, the accountant operating an accounting information system must perform a number of tasks. He or she must:

Create the system structure
    Design a chart of accounts
    Define the account categories

Process reports
    Prepare detailed reports
    (journals/ledger)
    Prepare summary reports
    (trial balance/financial statements)

Process source documents
    Analyze and code transactions
    Record transactions

Analyze results
    Prepare basic financial ratios
    Prepare special reports

The computer cannot help in all of these areas. As a matter of fact, if you think of the computer as a giant adding machine and typewriter, about all it can do is *process reports*. It certainly cannot tell you what account codes should be used in recording transactions. You must give the computer these instructions. And unless you are using an inflexible computer system preprogrammed with the system parameters, to some extent you will need to design and structure your own system.

Manual Accounting Systems

Manual accounting systems reflect our limitations in processing data without the aid of mechanical or electronic devices. Although these systems have evolved over hundreds of years, the basic procedures have remained the same. Manual systems are highly *sequential* in nature. Final results are available only after many steps are completed in a specific order. To modify or redo part of the process is either impossible or can be accomplished only in a later period.

The system begins with transaction analysis and eventually produces financial statements. Transactions are permanently *recorded* in a journal. Periodically, the journal entries are *classified* and transferred to the ledger by way of the posting process. The ledger transaction detail is then *summarized* by account to produce a list of account balances called a trial balance. Finally, the account balances are *categorized* or grouped for the financial statements.

Each step in the process must be completed in this order. The stair-step diagram implies a sequential, one-way progression. There is no backing up to a prior step.

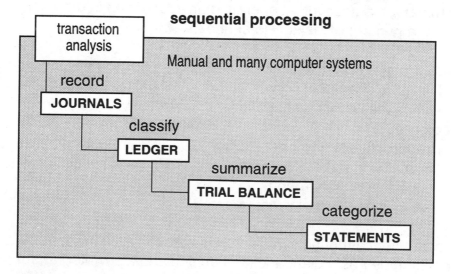

MANUAL ACCOUNTING SYSTEMS

sequential processing

transaction analysis

Manual and many computer systems

record

JOURNALS

classify

LEDGER

summarize

TRIAL BALANCE

categorize

STATEMENTS

Database Accounting Systems

Computer accounting systems can provide an opportunity to eliminate most of the limitations of the manual system. However, whether the system takes advantage of the computer usually depends on the designer's understanding of the limitations of the manual system. Often, the computer system is programmed as if it were a manual system, resulting in the same sequential processing.

As with the manual system, transactions must be analyzed before they can be entered into the system. However, once transactions are entered, there is no similarity between a manual system and a computer database system.

In a database system, new transactions are added to the *transaction database*. The computer can provide many views of the database contents on demand and in any order. This is called *random processing*. As shown in the diagram, there are no lines connecting the various reports or views of the database. For example, the income statement could be viewed after each transaction. This can be accomplished because the computer can complete in seconds a task that would otherwise take us hours or even days to complete.

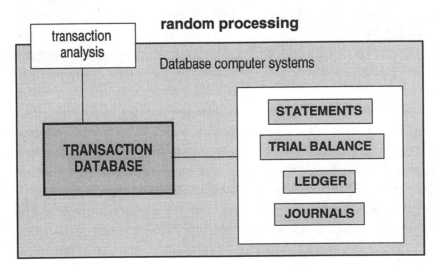

DATABASE ACCOUNTING SYSTEMS

Accounting Processing Steps

To be useful, data must be recorded, classified, summarized, categorized, and analyzed. Let's look at each step and compare the way it is done manually with the way a computer would do it.

RECORD ---------> JOURNALS

The act of recording data or observations is essential in all research. If we were collecting butterflies, we would record all pertinent data as each butterfly was received. We would note date, size, color, family, location, and other facts. It is the same with business transactions. Date, account code, amount, and explanation are all important.

In a manual system, transactions are permanently recorded in a paper journal. With a computer system, transactions are recorded directly on a storage device, such as a magnetic disk. Butterflies or business transactions, pen and paper or a magnetic disk, the process is really the same. The data are analyzed and *chronologically* recorded. This is the database used for all further processing.

CLASSIFY --------> LEDGER

To classify data means to *rearrange* or *sort* them by some attribute other than by the date they were recorded. How many ways could we classify butterflies? Attributes such as color, size, location, and family could all serve as classifications. How many ways do we classify business transactions? One way is by *account code.*

Rearrangement can take place *physically* or *logically*. If we added 100 butterflies a month to our collection, we would first analyze and record each one as it was received. We could physically arrange them by size and then possibly by color within size. The physical arrangements could have so many possibilities that it may be better to leave the butterflies in the order received and to rearrange them logically as needed. *Logical arrangement* takes place without physically moving or rearranging the database. It is relatively fast, and there is no possibility of losing data.

In the case of business transactions, source documents are physically filed in numerical order. The effects of the source documents are recorded in chronological order in a journal. In a manual system the entries in the journal are physically rearranged and transferred to a ledger. We call this *posting*. It is a process of physical rearrangement of data.

Generally, physical rearrangement is *time-consuming* and may result in *damage* or *loss* of accuracy. The more often butterflies are handled, the more likely that damage will occur. With posting, not all pertinent information is transferred to the ledger, resulting in a loss of usefulness. Most manual ledgers have a column for an explanation, but none is usually entered. The ledger consists of numbers providing little information to the user.

With a database accounting system, there is no physical movement of data. It is the logical views that provide the needed results. Logical processing is extremely fast and there is no loss of data. There are hundreds of logical views for the butterfly collector. It would not be practical to completely analyze the collection without the aid of the computer.

In summary, in a *manual system,* classification is a process called *posting*, which takes place by *physically* transferring the entries from the journal to the ledger. This is a very time-consuming process subject to errors and loss of pertinent data. In a *computer database system*, classification is a process of *logically* viewing data by account code. There is no movement or rearrangement of entries. It is fast and efficient without the loss of any data.

SUMMARIZE ------> TRIAL BALANCE

In the prior step of classification, all transactions were grouped by account code. To summarize simply means to total all entries in each account. After each account has been totaled, a list of all accounts with the account code, description, and debit or credit balance is prepared. This is called a trial balance.

Manually, this procedure is time consuming and is prone to error. If the trial balance is out of balance, it can provide more of a challenge than most of us are looking for. With a computer, a trial balance is just another view of the total transaction file. It is a summarized view of all transactions by account code.

CATEGORIZE ------> FINANCIAL STATEMENTS

A trial balance may be useful in an audit trail but accounts need to be grouped by family before relationships are evident. The balance sheet and income statement contain important *categories* used in financial analysis. For example, to calculate working capital, you must know which accounts are current assets and which are current liabilities. These categories are groupings of certain accounts.

In a manual system, this step takes time. With a computer, financial statements can be available almost instantly and at any time. The effects of certain decisions can be viewed as soon as the entry has been added to the database.

ANALYZE ---------> RATIOS

Often, the analysis of financial results is a matter of personal preference or style. However, ratios are often used as a means of highlighting trends. A *ratio* is simply the relationship between two numbers (one number divided by another number). The computer can provide many ratios as easily as it can provide the financial statements.

Visible Accounting Systems

Visible Accounting Systems, or VAS, is the accounting cycle portion of the software for the Computer Resource Guide (CRG). (For information on the electronic spreadsheet templates portion of the software, please see Part Two of this manual.) VAS is so named because the effect of any accounting entry is visible at any time. Please read the following instructions completely before you begin. When you have finished reading the instructions, you should be ready to load the computer and begin work on the sample problem (Westgate Driving School) that follows in Chapter 3.

Requirements

♦   IBM PC microcomputer and monitor (or IBM XT or IBM AT with 5 1/4-inch, 360 KB drive) **OR** IBM PS/2 with 3 1/2-inch, 720 KB drive. (This package is available from the publisher in both formats.)
♦   One double-sided disk drive.*
♦   256 K RAM of memory.
♦   PC DOS 2.1 or higher, referred to as the disk operating system.
♦   80-column, parallel printer if reports are to be printed.
    (Note: We cannot guarantee that VAS will work with a networked printer.)
    *VAS is not copy protected and should be run from a floppy disk drive that reads and writes at double density.

Program Execution and General Instructions

A. Load VAS - *Single Disk Drive Option*

   1. (a) Insert the operating system disk (DOS) in Drive A and close the disk drive door.
      (b) Boot the system by turning on the power (if not already on) or by depressing the **<Ctrl>** key, the **<Alt>** key, and the **<Del>** key simultaneously.
      (c) An on-screen message will ask you to enter the date and time. You may do so, or you may bypass these requests by pressing **<Enter>**. Note: The **<Enter>** key is the same as the **<Return>** key (left-pointing bent-arrow key).
      (d) When the computer is ready, the letter A followed by a *greater than* sign will appear on screen, as **A>**.
   2. (a) Remove DOS from Drive A and insert the CRG disk. Close the disk drive door.
      (b) Type **VAS** and press **<Enter>**. The VAS program will begin.

OR

A. Load <u>VAS</u> - *Double Disk Drive Option*
   (This is an option for those users whose machine has two disk drives and who prefer to keep DOS in Drive A. Obviously, a user with a double disk drive machine could still employ the single disk drive option outlined above.)
   1. (a) Insert the operating system disk (DOS) in Drive A and close the disk drive door.
      (b) Insert the *CRG* disk in Drive B and close the disk drive door.
      (c) Boot the system by turning on the power (if not already on) or by depressing the **<Ctrl>** key, the **<Alt>** key, and the **<Del>** key simultaneously.
      (d) An on-screen message will ask you to enter the date and time. You may do so, or you may bypass these requests by pressing **<Enter>**. <u>Note</u>: The **<Enter>** key is the same as the **<Return>** key (left-pointing bent-arrow key).
      (e) When the computer is ready, the letter <u>A</u> followed by a *greater than* sign will appear on screen, as **A>**.
   2. (a) Type **B:** and press **<Enter>**. (Be sure to include the colon after the letter <u>B</u>. You will need to depress the **<Shift>** key while you type the colon.)
      (b) The computer will now display the letter <u>B</u> followed by a greater than sign, as **B>**.
      (c) Type **VAS** after the B> and press **<Enter>**. The <u>VAS</u> program will begin.

B. When the <u>VAS</u> book appears on the screen, press any key to open it and to turn the copyright pages. If the disk has not been initialized, you will be asked to enter your name. At the COMPANY SELECTION page you will be asked to enter a single letter for the storage disk drive to be used. Enter the letter corresponding to the drive your program disk is in (A or B) **without** pressing the **<Enter>** key. Whenever a single character is required for an input, **do not** follow the input by the **<Enter>** key. After entering the disk drive letter, a list of available company files will be displayed in a window on the left page. Any file can be selected by first highlighting the name by pressing the arrow keys and then pressing the **<Enter>** key. Your disk may contain a company file named DEMO. You may wish to load this file and view its contents.

C. If you intend to create a new company file, you would press the letter **<C>** for CREATE when the available files are shown. Do not use periods, spaces or any special character as part of the file name. Data for many companies can be stored on the same disk by using a separate file name for each company. Enter the full company name and then press the **<Enter>** key.

D. Process the desired activity. (The Westgate Driving School sample problem that follows provides an excellent introduction to the system.)

NOTE: <u>Visible Accounting Systems</u> is designed to be activated by a single key stroke. The **<Enter>** key does not need to be pressed unless you are entering field values. All menu requests and question responses need only a single key stroke without pressing the **<Enter>** key.

The sample problem that follows consists of a transaction narrative, completed data entry forms, instructions, and solutions. In a real problem, you would prepare the data entry forms yourself. The purpose of this sample problem is to introduce the computer system.

Westgate Driving School
Transaction Narrative

EXPERIENCED DRIVER EDUCATION INSTRUCTOR JOHN KING ESTABLISHED A PRIVATE DRIVING SCHOOL CALLED WESTGATE DRIVING SCHOOL. KING INTENDS TO BUY A LOT FOR VEHICLE STORAGE AND DRIVER INSTRUCTION, BUT TO LEASE TRAINING VEHICLES. THE TRANSACTIONS FOR JUNE, THE FIRST MONTH OF OPERATIONS, ARE ANALYZED BELOW.

(1) On June 1, John King deposited $60,000 of his personal funds in a special checking account for the Westgate Driving School.

(2) On June 2, King paid $24,000 for a lot to be used for storing vehicles and for some driving instruction.

(3) On June 3, King paid $800 to rent a furnished office and $5,000 for leasing training vehicles for June.

(4) On June 4, King paid vehicle insurance premiums of $7,200 for three years.

(5) On June 5, King purchased fuel and other supplies on account for $3,600.

(6) On June 26, the school's students were billed $21,500 for June instructional fees.

(7) On June 30, King paid instructors' salaries of $9,000 for June .

(8) On June 30, the school collected $18,000 on account from students billed in transaction (6).

(9) On June 30, the school paid $1,600 on account for the supplies purchased in transaction (5).

(10) On June 30, King paid $250 for office utilities (electricity and telephone).

(11) On June 30, King withdrew $2,000 from the firm for personal use.

(12) On June 30, one month of the prepaid insurance, or $200, had expired.

(13) On June 30, supplies were counted, and only $1,350 worth of supplies remained on hand.

For this sample problem only, the following have been entered on the accompanying forms:

CATEGORY DEFINITIONS
CHART OF ACCOUNTS
TRANSACTION JOURNAL

Using the following instructions, install a computer system for Westgate Driving School and process the June transactions.

Instructions

Load the <u>Visible Accounting Systems</u> program using the instructions in Chapter 2.

ACCOUNTANT'S NAME
If the program has not already been initialized, you will be asked to enter your name for identification purposes. Verify that the name is correct by typing **<Y>**.

COMPANY SELECTION
You will be asked to enter the storage disk drive letter (A,B,C,etc.). Respond with the correct letter without pressing the **<Enter>** key. Whenever a single letter response is required, do not press the **<Enter>** key. Press **<C>** to create a new file.

COMPANY CODE
You will be asked to enter eight letters or fewer for a company *code*. Enter the code and then press **<Enter>** to indicate the end of the code. Use a code that is easy to remember such as WESTGATE, or WDS. The code must be used later when accessing the company's file. When entering company codes, use only letters. Do not use commas, periods, spaces, or any special characters.

COMPANY NAME
Enter the full company name exactly as you want it to appear on all reports. Press the **<Enter>** key to indicate the end of the name. You will then be asked if this name is correct. Respond with the letter **<Y>** without pressing the **<Enter>** key. Then you will be asked if this is the company you want to process. Press **<Y>** again.

The company has been established. You are now in charge of operating the system. You do this by selecting menu options that will direct the computer to perform certain operations.

INPUT MENU

Transactions cannot be added to the data base until the account categories have been defined and the accounts have been established.

Select the **INPUT** menu, at the bottom of the screen, by pressing **<2>** (for option 2) or **<I>** (for Input). Do not press the **<Enter>** key.
From the **INPUT** menu, select the account categories by pressing **<2>** or **<C>**.

ACCOUNT CATEGORIES

Using the accompanying form, enter the category definitions as follows:

Enter each account range or press **<Enter>** to skip to the next item.
Press the **<Escape>** key until you return to the main **MENU**, which displays the financial records book.

CHART OF ACCOUNTS

Using the accompanying form, enter the Chart of Accounts as follows:

Select the **INPUT** menu by pressing **<2>** or **<I>**.
Now select the chart of accounts by pressing **<3>** or **<A>**.
Enter the account number and press **<Enter>**.
Enter the Description and press **<Enter>**.
Continue with the next account. Accounts can be entered in any order.
If you make a mistake, press **<Escape>** and you will be given some options to make corrections.
Press the **<Escape>** key to return to the main **MENU**.

TRANSACTIONS

You are now ready to add transactions to the database as follows:

Select the **INPUT** menu by pressing **<2>** or **<I>**.
Now select the transactions journal by pressing **<4>** or **<T>**.
Name the journal **GJ1** and press **<Enter>**.
Enter the month and year (use 2 characters).
You will be asked if the JOURNAL and DATE are correct. Press **<Y>**.

Enter each line from the transaction journal form. You can duplicate a prior field (entry directly above) by pressing the **<Enter>** key. A credit amount can be duplicated from a prior debit amount by pressing the **<Enter>** key.

Press **<Escape>** to return to the main **MENU**.

Westgate Driving School

Category Definitions

BALANCE SHEET	BEG#	END#
A – Current Assets	100	159
B – Long-Term Assets	160	189
C – Other Assets		
D – Current Liabilities	200	249
E – Long-Term Liabilities		
F – Owner Equity	300	399

INCOME STATEMENT	BEG#	END#
G – Operating Revenues	400	499
H – Other Revenues		
I – Operating Costs		
J – Operating Expenses	500	599
k – Other Expenses		

Chart Of Accounts

ACCT	DESCRIPTION
100	Cash
120	Accounts Receivable
130	Prepaid Insurance
140	Supplies on Hand
160	Land
220	Accounts Payable
300	J. King, Capital
310	J. King, Drawing
400	Instructional Fees
510	Rent Expense
520	Salaries Expense
530	Utilities Expcnes
540	Insurance Expense
550	Supplies Expense

FINANCIAL SUMMARY

DATE: _____

Total Assets		
Total Liabilities		
Owner Equity		

Total Revenues		
Total Expenses		
Net Income		

SYSTEM DESIGNED BY:

Accountant		Date	

Westgate Driving School

Transaction Journal

JOUR | GJ1
MOYR | 06/93

DAY	ACCT	DESCRIPTION	DEBIT	CREDIT	EXPLANATION
01	100	Cash	60,000		Initial investment
01	300	J. King, Capital		60,000	"
02	160	Land	24,000		Vacant lot
02	100	Cash		24,000	"
03	510	Rent Expense	5,8000		June rent
03	100	Cash		5,800	"
04	130	Prepaid Insurance	7,200		3 year insurance policy
04	100	Cash		7,200	"
05	140	Supplies on Hand	3,600		Fuel and supplies
05	220	Accounts Payable		3,600	"
26	120	Accounts Receivable	21,500		June billings
26	400	Instructional Fees		21,500	"
30	520	Salaries Expense	9,000		June salaries
30	100	Cash		9,000	"
30	100	Cash	18,000		Collect on account
30	120	Accounts Receivable		18,000	"
30	220	Accounts Payable	1,600		Paid on account
30	100	Cash		1,600	"
30	530	Utilities Expense	250		Electric and phone
30	100	Cash		250	"
30	310	J. King, Drawing	2,000		Personal draw
30	100	Cash		2,000	"
30	540	Insurance expense	200		June insurance
30	130	Prepaid Insurance		200	"
30	550	Supplies Expense	2,250		Supplies used in June
30	140	Supplies on Hand		2,250	"

Accountant | | Date |

AUDIT

Reports can be viewed at any time and in any order. When the records are audited, the relationships between reports will be highlighted. These highlighted relationships visually display the *audit trail,* which links all of the reports together. For example, if you highlight an account on the trial balance and then press the **<Left>** arrow key to move back to the general ledger, the transactions for the same account will be displayed as part of the General Ledger. If you then highlight a transaction in this ledger account and press the **<Left>** arrow key, you will move backward to the journal containing the corresponding entry, which will also be highlighted.

Select the **AUDIT** menu by pressing **<3>** or **<A>**.
Select the REPORT to audit by pressing the number or first letter of the desired report.

Using the audit options shown on the menu bar at the bottom of the screen, explore the relationships between the reports. Compare your results with the sample printed reports for Westgate Driving School that follow. If you have any errors, use the modify options for either accounts or transactions, or check your account category definitions.

PRINT

Reports can be generated at any time without regard to the order of reporting. For example, the financial statements can be produced without first running a trial balance.

Select the **PRINT** menu by pressing **<4>** or **<P>**.
Select the REPORT to print by pressing the appropriate number or first letter.

You are now ready to use the system on a number of different problems. Before you begin Chapter 5, Practical Problem Applications, however, you may wish to learn more about this system by reading the detailed description of menu operations given in Chapter 4.

Solutions to the Westgate Driving School Problem

Solutions to the problem are reproduced on the following pages.

```
                    Westgate Driving School
                      FINANCIAL ANALYSIS
                 June 1, 1995  To  June 30, 1995

===================================================================
         BALANCE SHEET                   INCOME STATEMENT
-------------------------------------------------------------------
ASSETS:                          REVENUES:
A - Current Assets      40,000.00 G - Operating Revenues   21,500.00
B - Long-Term Assets    24,000.00 H - Other Revenues            0.00
C - Other Assets             0.00                          -----------
                       -----------                          21,500.00
      Total             64,000.00 COSTS AND EXPENSES:
                       ===========  I - Operating Costs          0.00
                                    J - Operating Expenses  17,500.00
LIABILITIES AND EQUITIES:          K - Other Expenses           0.00
D - Current Liabilities  2,000.00                          -----------
E - Long-Term Liabilities    0.00                           17,500.00
                       -----------
                         2,000.00  SUMMARY OF INCOME:
F - Owner Equity        58,000.00     Operating Income       4,000.00
    Net Income (Loss)    4,000.00 <<<  Other Income (Loss)       0.00
                       -----------                         -----------
      Total             64,000.00  <<< Net Income (Loss)     4,000.00
                       ===========                         ===========


-------------------------------------------------------------------
       SOLVENCY ANALYSIS              PROFITABILITY ANALYSIS
-------------------------------------------------------------------
Current Assets      40,000.00    Total Revenues    21,500.00 100.0%
Current Liabilities  2,000.00    Operating Costs        0.00   0.0%
Working Capital     38,000.00                      -----------
Current Ratio      20.00 to 1    Gross Margin      21,500.00 100.0%
Total Liabilities  2,000.00  3.1% Total Expenses   17,500.00  81.4%
Owner  Equity     62,000.00 96.9%                  -----------
Total Assets      64,000.00 100.0% Net Income (Loss) 4,000.00  18.6%


-------------------------------------------------------------------
               COMBINED RELATIONAL ANALYSIS
-------------------------------------------------------------------
  Net Income    Total Revenues   Net Income   Owner Equity   Net Income
------------- x -------------- = ------------ / ------------ = ------------
Total Revenues  Total Assets    Total Assets   Total Assets  Owner Equity
    ||               ||              ||              ||            ||
    \/               \/              \/              \/            \/
 Profit Margin  Asset Turnover  Asset Return   Equity Ratio  Equity Return
    18.6%     x    0.34 times  =    6.3%     /    96.9%    =     6.5%

===================================================================
```

```
                Westgage Driving School
                     BALANCE SHEET
                    June 30, 1995

ASSETS
---------------------------------

Current Assets
   Cash                          28,150.00
   Account Receivable             3,500.00
   Prepaid Insurance              7,000.00
   Supplies on Hand               1,350.00
                                --------------      40,000.00
Long-Term Assets
   Land                          24,000.00
                                --------------      24,000.00
                                                --------------
                                                    64,000.00
                                                ==============


LIABILITIES AND EQUITIES
---------------------------------

Current Liabilities
   Account Payable                2,000.00
                                --------------       2,000.00
Owner Equity
   J. King, Capital              60,000.00
   J. King, Drawing              -2,000.00
   Net Income (Loss)              4,000.00
                                --------------      62,000.00
                                                --------------
                                                    64,000.00
                                                ==============

                Westgage Driving School
                    INCOME STATEMENT
            June 01, 1995  To  June 30, 1995

REVENUES
---------------------------------

Operating Revenues
   Instructional Fees            21,500.00
                                --------------      21,500.00

COSTS, EXPENSES
---------------------------------

Operating Expenses
   Rent Expense                   5,800.00
   Salaries Expense               9,000.00
   Utilities Expense                250.00
   Insurance Expense                200.00
   Supplies Expense               2,250.00
                                --------------      17,500.00
                                                --------------
Operating Net Income (Loss)                          4,000.00
                                                ==============
```

Westgage Driving School
TRIAL BALANCE
June 01, 1995 To June 30, 1995

ACCT	DESCRIPTION	DEBIT	CREDIT	ENTRIES
100	Cash	28,150.00		9
120	Account Receivable	3,500.00		2
130	Prepaid Insurance	7,000.00		2
140	Supplies on Hand	1,350.00		2
160	Land	24,000.00		1
220	Accounts Payable		2,000.00	2
300	J. King, Capital		60,000.00	1
310	J. King, Drawing	2,000.00		1
400	Instructional Fees		21,500.00	1
510	Rent Expense	5,800.00		1
520	Salaries Expense	9,000.00		1
530	Utilities Expense	250.00		1
540	Insurance Expense	200.00		1
550	Supplies Expense	2,250.00		1

BALANCE	0.00	TOTALS	83,500.00	83,500.00	26

Westgate Driving School

ACCOUNT CATEGORIES

BALANCE SHEET	BEG#	END#
A - Current Assets	100	159
B - Long-Term Assets	160	189
C - Other Assets	0	0
D - Current Liabilities	200	249
E - Long-Term Liabilities	0	0
F - Owner Equity	300	399

INCOME STATEMENT	BEG#	END#
G - Operating Revenues	400	499
H - Other Revenues	0	0
I - Operating Costs	0	0
J - Operating Expense	500	599
K - Other Expense	0	0

CHART OF ACCOUNTS
ACCOUNT CATEGORIES

A - Current Assets		100	159
	100	Cash	
	120	Accounts Receivable	
	130	Prepaid Insurance	
	140	Supplies on Hand	

B - Long-Term Assets		160	189
	160	Land	

D - Current Liabilities		200	249
	220	Accounts Payable	

F - Owner Equity		300	399
	300	J. King, Capital	
	310	J. King, Drawing	

G - Operating Revenues		400	499
	400	Instructional Fees	

J - Operating Expenses		500	599
	510	Rent Expense	
	520	Salaries Expense	
	530	Utilities Expense	
	540	Insurance Expense	
	550	Supplies Expense	

Westgate Drive School
TRANSACTION JOURNALS
June 01, 1995 To June 30, 1995

ACCOUNT: 100 Cash

MO DA YR	JOUR	EXPLANATION	DEBIT	CREDIT	BALANCE
06-01-95	GJ1	Initial Investment	60,000.00		60,000.00
06-02-95	GJ1	Vacant Lot		24,000.00	36,000.00
06-03-95	GJ1	June Rent		5,800.00	30,200.00
06-04-95	GJ1	3 Year Policy		7,200.00	23,000.00
06-30-95	GJ1	June Salaries		9,000.00	14,000.00
06-30-95	GJ1	Collect on Account	18,000.00		32,000.00
06-30-95	GJ1	Paid on Account		1,600.00	30,400.00
06-30-95	GJ1	Electric and Phone		250.00	30,150.00
06-30-95	GJ1	Personal Draw		2,000.00	28,150.00

ACCOUNT: 120 Accounts Receivable

MO DA YR	JOUR	EXPLANATION	DEBIT	CREDIT	BALANCE
06-26-95	GJ1	June Billings	21,500.00		21,500.00
06-30-95	GJ1	Collect on Account		18,000.00	3,500.00

ACCOUNT: 130 Prepaid Insurance

MO DA YR	JOUR	EXPLANATION	DEBIT	CREDIT	BALANCE
06-04-95	GJ1	3 Year Policy	7,200.00		7,200.00
06-30-95	GJ1	June Insurance		200.00	7,000.00

ACCOUNT: 140 Supplies on Hand

MO DA YR	JOUR	EXPLANATION	DEBIT	CREDIT	BALANCE
06-05-95	GJ1	Fuel and Supplies	3,600.00		3,600.00
06-30-95	GJ1	Supplies used in June		2,250.00	1,350.00

ACCOUNT: 160 Land

MO DA YR	JOUR	EXPLANATION	DEBIT	CREDIT	BALANCE
06-02-95	GJ1	Vacant Land	24,000.00		24,000.00

ACCOUNT: 220 Accounts Payable

MO DA YR	JOUR	EXPLANATION	DEBIT	CREDIT	BALANCE
06-05-95	GJ1	Fuel and Supplies		3,600.00	3,600.00 C
06-30-95	GJ1	Paid on Account	1,600.00		2,000.00 C

ACCOUNT: 300 J. King, Capital

MO DA YR	JOUR	EXPLANATION	DEBIT	CREDIT	BALANCE
06-01-95	GJ1	Initial Investment		60,000.00	60,000.00 C

ACCOUNT: 310 J. King, Drawing

MO DA YR JOUR	EXPLANATION	DEBIT	CREDIT	BALANCE
06-30-95 GJ1	Personal Draw	2,000.00		2,000.00

ACCOUNT: 400 Instructional Fees

MO DA YR JOUR	EXPLANATION	DEBIT	CREDIT	BALANCE
06-26-95 GJ1	June Billing		21,500.00	21,500.00C

ACCOUNT: 510 Rent Expense

MO DA YR JOUR	EXPLANATION	DEBIT	CREDIT	BALANCE
06-03-95 GJ1	June Rent	5,800.00		5,800.00

ACCOUNT: 520 Salaries Expense

MO DA YR JOUR	EXPLANATION	DEBIT	CREDIT	BALANCE
06-02-95 GJ1	June Salaries	9,000.00		9,000.00

ACCOUNT: 530 Utilities Expense

MO DA YR JOUR	EXPLANATION	DEBIT	CREDIT	BALANCE
06-02-95 GJ1	Electric and Phone	250.00		250.00

ACCOUNT: 540 Insurance Expense

MO DA YR JOUR	EXPLANATION	DEBIT	CREDIT	BALANCE
06-02-95 GJ1	June Insurance	200.00		200.00

ACCOUNT: 550 Supplies Expense

MO DA YR JOUR	EXPLANATION	DEBIT	CREDIT	BALANCE
06-02-95 GJ1	Supplies used in June	2,250.00		2,250.00

```
                        Westgate Driving School
                          TRANSACTION JOURNALS
                    June 01, 1995  To  June 30, 1995

JOUR: GJ     DATE: 06/95
===========================================================================
DA ACCT DESCRIPTION              DEBIT        CREDIT    EXPLANATION
---------------------------------------------------------------------------
01 100  Cash                     60,000.00              Initial Investment
01 300  J. King, Capital                     60,000.00  Initial Investment
02 160  Land                     24,000.00              Vacant Lot
02 100  Cash                                 24,000.00  Vacant Lot
03 510  Rent Expense              5,800.00              June Rent
03 100  Cash                                  5,800.00  June Rent
04 130  Prepaid Insurance         7,200.00              3 Year Policy
04 100  Cash                                  7,200.00  3 Year Policy
05 140  Supplies on Hand          3,600.00              Fuel and Supplies
05 220  Accounts Payable                      3,600.00  Fuel and Supplies
26 120  Accounts Receivable      21,500.00              June Billings
26 400  Instructional Fees                   21,500.00  June Billings
30 520  Salaries Expense          9,000.00              June Salaries
30 100  Cash                                  9,000.00  June Salaries
30 100  Cash                     18,000.00              Collect on Account
30 120  Accounts Receivable                  18,000.00  Collect on Account
30 220  Accounts Payable          1,600.00              Paid on Account
30 100  Cash                                  1,600.00  Paid on Account
30 530  Utilities Expense           250.00              Electric and Phone
30 100  Cash                                    250.00  Electric and Phone
30 310  J. King, Drawing          2,000.00              Personal Draw
30 100  Cash                                  2,000.00  Personal Draw
30 540  Insurance Expense           200.00              June Insurance
30 130  Prepaid Insurance                       200.00  June Insurance
30 550  Supplies Expense          2,250.00              Supplies used in June
30 140  Supplies on Hand                      2,250.00  Supplies used in June
---------------------------------------------------------------------------
ENTRIES   26     TOTALS         155,400.00  155,400.00  BALANCE        0.00
===========================================================================
```

The <u>VAS</u> software program is easy to learn and intutitive to use. The operating instructions in Chapter 2 and the sample problem in Chapter 3 are designed to provide a quick introduction to the system. After completing the sample problem, you may want to review the various options that are outlined in this chapter. Most of the information outlined here is available while running the program, either in the form of an on-line help booklet or as a prompt at the bottom of the display screen.

The IBM microcomputer contains a number of special keys that will be used to navigate through the system and enter data. Generally, these keystrokes fall into two categories: keystrokes allowing you to highlight certain items on the screen and keystrokes allowing you to input and edit data fields. These are outlined below:

Highlight / Selection Keystrokes

<Home>	Move to the top of the list
<PgUp>	Move up one page
<Up>	Move up one line (up arrow key)
<Down>	Move down one line (down arrow key)
<PgDn>	Move down one page
<End>	Move to the bottom of the list
<Ctrl-Home>	Move to the first group (journals, ledger account, category)
<Ctrl-PgUp>	Move to the prior group (journals, ledger account, category)
<Ctrl-PgDn>	Move to the next group (journals, ledger account, category)
<Ctrl-End>	Move to the last group (journals, ledger account, category)
<Esc>	Back up to the prior operation

Data Entry / Edit Keystrokes

<Del>	Delete the current character
<Backspace> ...	Delete the prior character
<Ins>	Toggle the insert/overwrite option
<Left>	Move one character left (left arrow key)
<Right>	Move one character right (right arrow key)
<Home>	Move to the first character
<End>	Move to the last character
<Enter>	Accept the field data and move forward
<Esc>	Back up to the prior operation

Visible Accounting Systems
Menu Relationships

MENU / Submenus

---

1 - HELP

---

2 - INPUT

    1 - HELP ....Help on using the options in Input
    2 - CATEGORIES ....Create and modify account **CATEGORIES**
    3 - ACCOUNTS ....Add, modify, or delete **ACCOUNTS**
    4 - TRANSACTIONS ....Add, modify, or delete **TRANSACTIONS**
                     or create a new journal

---

3 - AUDIT

    1 - HELP ....Help on using the options in Audit
    2 - COA ....View categories and **C**hart **O**f **A**ccounts
    3 - JOUR ....View a summary and/or individual **JOUR**nals
    4 - GLED ....View the **G**eneral **LED**ger
    5 - TBAL ....View the **T**rial **BAL**ance
    6 - ACAT ....View the detail of **A**ccount **CAT**egories
    7 - STAT ....View the financial **STAT**ements
    8 - RATS ....View financial **RAT**ios/analysi**S**

---

4 - PRINT

    1 - HELP ....Help on using the options in Print
    2 - COA ....Print the categories and **C**hart **O**f **A**ccounts
    3 - JOUR ....Print the **JOUR**nals
    4 - GLED ....Print the **G**eneral **LED**ger
    5 - TBAL ....Print a **T**rial **BAL**ance
    6 - BS ....Print a **B**alance **S**heet
    7 - IS ....Print an **I**ncome **S**tatement
    8 - SUMM ....Print a financial **SUMM**ary
    9 - ALL ....Print **ALL** reports in sequence

---

5 - QUIT ....End system and save current work

COMPANY SELECTION

The company selection screen allows you to select a storage disk drive to use. Press a single letter (<u>A</u>, <u>B</u>, etc.) and wait while the data files are read from the designated drive. If any data files are found, they are displayed in a window. Use the **<Up>**, **<Down>** arrow keys to highlight a file and then press **<Enter>** to select the file. If you want to create a new file, press the letter **<C>** for create and then enter the new file name and the full company name.

MENU

1 - HELP

From the MENU screen press **<F1>**, **<1>**, or **<H>** to display a help booklet. The information is arranged by topic. Use the **<Up>**, **<Down>** keys or press a number to view any topic. When finished, press **<Esc>** to remove the booklet and return to your work.

2 - INPUT

From the MENU screen press **<F2>**, **<2>**, or **<I>** to display the INPUT menu. The INPUT menu has four options: 1-HELP, 2-CATEGORIES, 3-ACCOUNTS, and 4-TRANSACTIONS. This menu allows you to establish the accounting system by defining the account categories and maintaining the chart of accounts. Using the TRANSACTIONS option, you will maintain the transaction database. The INPUT options are expalined in the following section.

3 - AUDIT

From the MENU screen press **<F3>**, **<3>**, or **<A>** to display the AUDIT menu. The AUDIT menu has eight options: 1-HELP, 2-COA, 3-JOUR, 4-GLED, 5-TBAL, 6-ACAT, 7-STAT, AND 8-RATS. This menu allows you to view the financial records while actively selecting the audit trail path. By highlighting direct relationships between the reports, you will clearly see how the detailed business transactions are recorded, classified, and then summarized. The electronic audit trail will provide you with power not available with a manual system. The AUDIT options are explained in the following section.

4 - PRINT

From the MENU screen press **<F4>**, **<4>**, or **<P>** to display the PRINT menu. The PRINT menu has nine options: 1-HELP, 2-COA, 3-JOUR, 4-GLED, 5-TBAL, 6-BS, 7-IS, 8-SUMM, and 9-ALL. This menu allows you to print individual reports or all reports. The PRINT options are explained in the following section.

5 - QUIT

The QUIT option ends the system and saves your work.

2 - CATEGORIES

Highlight a category and then choose an option.

<M>odify .... <u>Type up to 4 characters or just **<Enter>** to skip.</u>
Type the beginning account code for the appropriate category and then press **<Enter>**. Then type the ending account code for that category. Press **<Enter>** and you will be moved automatically to the next category. Press **<Esc>** at any time to back up to the **<M>**odify option.

<Esc> .... Back up to INPUT choices

Accounts must be grouped into meaningful categories to produce the financial statements. The categories shown below are used for this purpose.

<u>Current Assets</u> include cash and other assets that will be converted to cash within the normal accounting cycle or one year, whichever is longer. Accounts receivable, inventory, short-term notes receivable, and prepaid expenses are usually included in this category.

<u>Long-Term Assets</u> are noncurrent assets with a life of more than one year and used in operating the business. Land, buildings, equipment and other depreciable assets are included in this category. The accumulated depreciation related to these accounts is also included in this category.

<u>Other Assets</u> are assets that are not used in operating the business. Investment in assets that are not directly related to the main business activity, such as real estate, stocks, or bonds would be included.

<u>Current Liabilities</u> are liabilities that are due within the normal operating cycle or one year, whichever is longer. Accounts payable, accrued payables, income or property taxes payable, and short-term notes payable would be included. Unearned revenue (amounts received from customers before earning the revenue) would also be included.

<u>Long-Term Liabilities</u> are liabilities that are not due for a relatively long time, usually more than one year. Mortages, long-term notes, and contracts payable would be included.

<u>Owner Equity</u> is the owner's share of the assets. It would include the capital and drawing accounts for a sole proprietorship or partnership and the stock and retained earnings accounts for a corporation.

<u>Operating Revenues</u> include all revenue from operating the business either from sale of a product or fees earned from selling a service.

<u>Other Revenues</u> are revenues from activities not directly related to the operations of the business. Interest income and gain on sale of long-term assets are two examples.

<u>Operating Costs</u> include all accounts related to the cost of goods sold. Purchases, transportation-in, and purchases returns are a few examples. It will be helpful to include an account for beginning inventory and one for ending inventory also. This category does not need to be defined unless the business sells a product.

<u>Operating Expenses</u> include all expenses directly related to operating the business. General, selling, and administrative expenses are all included.

<u>Other Expenses</u> are expenses not directly related to operating the business. Examples are interest expense and loss on sale of long-term assets.

INPUT MENU

3 - ACCOUNTS

Highlight an account and/or choose an option.

<A>dd .... <u>Type an account code of 4 characters or less.</u>
Accounts will be entered at the bottom of the account list.
When complete, the account will be automatically inserted
in the proper sequence. The account code may consist of letters
or numbers. When the account code is entered, the
corresponding category will also be highlighted. Duplicate
account codes are not allowed. Account codes that are not
included in an account category are not allowed. Press **<Enter>**
to accept.

<u>Type the account description.</u>
Type up to 30 characters for the account description; then press
<Enter> to accept or **<Esc>** to back up to the account code.

<M>odify .... <u>Type the account description.</u>
Only the account description can be modified. If an account code
is inactive (no transactions in the database), it can be deleted and
a new account can be entered.

<D>elete .... Respond to one of the messages:

<u>The account has active transactions and cannot be deleted, OK?</u>
Only accounts that have not be used in the transaction file
(inactive accounts) can be deleted.
     or
<u>Are you sure you want to delete the highlighted account?</u>

In either case, press **<Y>** to confirm or **<N>** or **<Esc>** to ignore.

<Esc> ....Back up to INPUT choices

4 - TRANSACTIONS

Highlight an entry and then choose an option
(Use **<Ctrl-PgUp>**, **<Ctrl-PgDn>**, **<Ctrl-Home>**, or **<Ctrl-End>** to turn journal pages.)

<A>dd .... This option allows entries to be added to an existing journal. Transactions will be added after the highlighted line. The following five fields will be requested.

DA .... Type 2 characters for the day (01-31) or **<Enter>** to duplicate. When this field is blank, press **<Enter>** to duplicate the day from the previous line.

ACCT .... Type 4 characters or less. After typing the account code, press **<Enter>** to accept. If the account is valid the description will be automatically displayed, otherwise, the chart of accounts will be displayed in a pop-up window. To select an account from the pop-up window, highlight the account and press **<Enter>** or press **<Esc>** to remove the window. If this field is blank, simply press **<Enter>** to display the chart of accounts window.

DEBIT .... Type the debit amount or press **<Enter>** to move to the credit column. Commas and cents will be automatically formatted and displayed after the **<Enter>** key is pressed. For example, to enter $1,250.00, type 1250 without commas or cents. To enter $75.50 type 75.5 without the last zero.

CREDIT .... Type the credit amount or **<Enter>** to duplicate prior debit. When this field is blank, press **<Enter>** to duplicate the debit amount from the previous line.

EXPLANATION ..... Type explanation or **<Enter>** to duplicate. When this field is blank, press **<Enter>** to duplicate the explanation from the prior line.

NOTE: For any of the above fields, press **<Esc>** to back up to the prior field.

4 - TRANSACTIONS   (continued)

<M>odify .... This option allows existing entries to be modified. First, highlight the entry to be modified and then press **<M>**. Enter the same fields as shown in the **<A>dd** option. Type new data or simply press **<Enter>** to duplicate the existing data.

<C>reate .... This option allows a new journal to be created. The following information will be requested.

    JOUR .... <u>Type up to 4 characters for the journal code.</u>
        Use any code, 4 characters or less, that will help identify the nature of the transactions. For example, TB could be used to indicate entries from an opening Trial Balance; CR for cash receipts, and so on.

    DATE .... <u>Type 2 characters for the month (01-12).</u>

        <u>Type 2 characters for the year (80-99).</u>

    The **JOUR** and **DATE** combination must be unique; duplicates are not allowed. This information cannot be changed after transactions have been entered. After the **JOUR** and **DATE** have been verified, transactions are entered using the same fields as described in the **<A>**dd option.

<Esc> .... Back up to INPUT choices

Reports can be viewed at any time and in any order. When the records are audited, the relationships between reports will be highlighted. These highlighted relationships visually display the *audit trail* which links all of the reports together. For example, if you highlight an account on the Trial Balance and then press the **<Left>** arrow key to move back to the general ledger, the transactions for the same account will be displayed as part of the general ledger. If you then highlight a transaction in this ledger account and press the **<Left>** arrow key, you will move backward to the journal containing the corresponding entry, which will also be highlighted. The report relationships are as follows:

2 - COA .... View categories and **C**hart **O**f **A**ccounts

3 - JOUR .... View a summary and/or individual **JOUR**nals

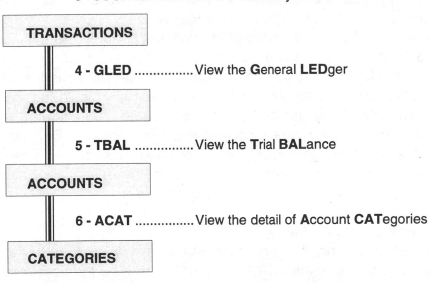

4 - GLED .... View the **G**eneral **LED**ger

5 - TBAL .... View the **T**rial **BAL**ance

6 - ACAT .... View the detail of **A**ccount **CAT**egories

7 - STAT .... View the financial **STAT**ements

8 - RATS .... View financial **RAT**ios/analysi**S**

2 - COA ....View categories and **Chart Of Accounts**

Highlight an account and press the **<Right>** arrow key to view the category group. Highlight a category to view the related accounts.

3 - JOUR .....View a journal summary or individual **JOUR**nals

Highlight a journal entry and press the **<Right>** arrow key to view the same entry as part of a general ledger account.

4 - GLED .....View the **General LED**ger

Highlight a ledger entry and press the **<Left>** arrow key to view the same entry as part of a journal. The ledger option reports transactions in the three-column format with a running balance after each entry. Although the format is identical to most manual ledgers, the content is not. Manual ledgers often provide a column for a description or explanation, but none is usually entered. In other words, usually no explanation is transferred from the journal to the ledger as part of the posting process. Because of this, the *manual ledger* consists mainly of numbers and is a cryptic and uninformative report. There is no quick visual way to determine the correctness of the account coding. There is no audit trail from the ledger directly to source documents.

Using the computer, the explanation column in the ledger contains all information that is recorded in the journals. The ledger becomes a focal point for analysis and review of all business activity. What a tremendous difference this makes. The *ledger* becomes a very important *management tool*. For example, when you are reviewing the expense accounts, each account contains all pertinent information such as the check or voucher number, supplier's name, and date. Many errors in account coding readily stand out.

5 - TBAL ......View the **T**rial **BAL**ance

Highlight an account and then press the **<Left>** arrow key to view the ledger detail for the account or press the **<Right>** arrow key to view the account as part of an account category. The journal and the ledger are both detailed reports of the transactions. The trial balance is a *summary report* of account balances as of a certain date. The format contains a debit and a credit column as well as a column for the number of entries in each account. This can be helpful in determining the activity for a particular account.

6 - ACAT ..... View the detail of **A**ccount **CAT**egories

Highlight an account and then press the **<Left>** arrow key to view the trial balance or press the **<Right>** arrow key to view the related category on the financial statements.

7 - STAT ...... View the financial **STAT**ements

This option reports the balance sheet and the income statement together summarized by categories. The 11 categories are represented by the letters <u>A</u> through <u>K</u>. The accounts contained in these categories have been defined by the user. Highlight a category, or simply press the category letter, to view the individual accounts for that category. The net income or Loss is shown on both reports to emphasize the *relationship* of the *income statement* to the *balance sheet*. In order to maintain a balance, the income statement must be reflected in the balance sheet in the form of the net income or loss. In effect, the entire income statement is a reflection of the owner equity activity. Without the netIncome or loss, it is visually clear that the balance sheet would be incomplete or out of balance.

8 - RATS ..... View financial **RAT**ios/analysi**S**

The financial statements provide basic <u>information</u> relative to the financial position (assets, liabilities, etc.) and the results of operations (net income or loss). However, information must be interpreted before effective decisions can be made. *Relationships* between accounts and categories can suggest important trends that are otherwise not visible.

Financial statement analysis can be very complex, requiring a great deal of knowledge of the particular company as well as the industry in which it operates. For our purposes, some basic relationships are essential in understanding and predicting financial trends.

Solvency and *profitability* are both critical to the well-being of a company. One does not ensure the other. For example, the more profitable the company, the more difficult it may be to remain solvent. Solvency analysis usually focuses on the balance sheet, and it is a measure of the ability of the company to pay debts as they become due.

Both *working capital* and *current ratio* are commonly used to measure a company's solvency. Current assets are related to current liabilities in at least two ways. By subtracting current liabilities from current assets, an amount called *working capital* is determined. This is a measure of the funds available to operate the company after payment of current debt. By dividing current assets by current liabilities, a relationship called *current ratio* is determined. This is a relative measure of the ability to pay current debts.

Profitability analysis starts with the income statement. Analysis of net iincome or loss by itself is not as helpful as when it is related to other categories. There are three very important relationships for *net income*. They are total revenues, total assets, and owner equity. There are three important relationships for *total assets*. They are total revenues, net income, and owner equity.

Together, total assets and net income combine to form five very interdependent relationships: profit margin, asset turnover, asset return, equity ratio, and equity return.

SOME BASIC FINANCIAL RELATIONSHIPS

$$\frac{\text{Net Income}}{\text{Total Revenues}}$$ = Profit Margin - Level of Profits per Sales Dollar.

X

$$\frac{\text{Total Revenues}}{\text{Total Assets}}$$ = Asset Turnover - Productivity of Assets or Volume of Sales.

=

$$\frac{\text{Net Income}}{\text{Total Assets}}$$ = Return on Assets - Income per Dollar of Assets.

/

$$\frac{\text{Owner Equity}}{\text{Total Assets}}$$ = Equity Ratio - Percent of Invested Assets.

=

$$\frac{\text{Net Income}}{\text{Owner Equity}}$$ = Return on Equity - Income per Dollar of Investment.
(Return on investment)

The profit margin multiplied by the asset turnover yields the return on assets. Some companies have a very small profit margin and a very high asset turnover. Because of the high volume of business, they may command a reasonable return on the owner's investment.

Other companies may have a very large profit margin yet a very small asset turnover. Because of the low volume of business, they may not yield an adequate return on the owner's investment.

The return on assets divided by the equity ratio yields the return on equity. The return on equity is often referred to as <u>return on investment</u> or simply **ROI**. For many, this is the ultimate test of a company's operations. How did the company do in relationship to the investment in the company? If the results fall short of expectations, then a complete analysis of all relevant facts is needed to pinpoint the problem areas.

In summary, financial analysis is critical in the decision-making process. Many approaches can be used, depending on one's background and understanding of the problems involved. The computer can provide the basic financial information and some analysis, but only the user can draw the appropriate conclusions.

PRINT MENU

Reports can be printed at any time and in any order. Use the following to print the desired report.

2 - COA ....Print the categories and **C**hart **O**f **A**ccounts

3 - JOUR ....Print the **JOUR**nals

4 - GLED ....Print the **G**eneral **LED**ger

5 - TBAL ....Print a **T**rial **BAL**ance

6 - BS ....Print a **B**alance **S**heet

7 - IS ....Print an **I**ncome **S**tatement

8 - SUMM ....Print a financial **SUMM**ary

9 - ALL ....Print **ALL** reports in sequence

Suggested Procedures

Each problem consists of the following:

(1) Problem setting, transaction narrative, beginning balances, adjustment information, and instructions as appropriate.

(2) Category Definitions and the Chart of Accounts form.

(3) Transaction Journal form for recording of transactions.
Note: Forms are grouped at the back of this manual.

The following procedures are recommended.

(A) *Remove the pertinent forms and place in front of you.* Then read the problem.

If the problem contains beginning balances, write your account numbers next to the account name or balance *on the problem narrative*, rather than recording the accounts and balances on the transaction journal. *Beginning balances* will be entered into the system as *transactions,* but this will save time because they can be entered directly from the opening trial balance.

(B) *Fill in the forms.*

The Chart of Accounts can be developed as you analyze and record transactions on the Transaction Journal. As each transaction is analyzed the need for a certain account will become evident. This interaction between the transactions and the need for account codes will help you develop both the Transaction Journal and the Chart of Accounts.

The Category Definitions can be defined *before*, *during*, or *after* the transactions have been analyzed and recorded. It really is a matter of preference. If defined beforehand, they will provide a framework for the Chart of Accounts. Experiment to find what is best for you. After all, you are the designer of the system, and designers have individual style.

(C) *Enter the data.*

Using the completed forms, you are now ready to use the computer for what it can do best: rapidly process data according to your directions. The sequence of data entry should be as follows:

INPUT CATEGORIES
The categories must be entered before the chart of accounts can be entered.

INPUT ACCOUNTS
The chart ofaccounts must be entered before transactions can be entered.

INPUT TRANSACTIONS
The computer can immediately provide the results of your decisions. If you discover that you must modify a transaction or rework your category definitions, you can do so instantly.

(D) *Store the data.*

When you are finished, don't forget to select QUIT from the MENU, so that the computer will file on the disk the data that you have entered.

(E) *Report final results.*

When you are satisfied with the results, complete the <u>Financial Summary</u> section of the system design form. This section is just below the category definitions. Depending on the availability of a printer, you may want to print reports for a permanent record.

James Behm, Contractor

2-29

James Behm, electrical contractor, began business on May 1, 1993. The following transactions occurred during May:

Day
1. Behm invested $20,000 of his personal funds in the business.
2. Purchased equipment on account, $3,500.
3. Returned $200 of equipment that was not satisfactory. The return reduced the amount owed to the supplier.
4. Purchased supplies on account, $920.
5. Purchased a truck for $10,500. Behm paid $4,500 cash and gave a note payable for the balance.
6. Paid rent for May, $825.
7. Paid fuel cost for truck, $80.
8. Billed customers for services rendered, $12,400.
9. Paid $2,000 on account for equipment purchased on May 2.
10. Paid cost of utilities for May, $180.
12. Received invoice for May advertising, to be paid in June, $250.
15. Paid employees' wages, $3,150.
21. Collected $7,200 on accounts receivable.
30. Behm withdrew $900 for personal expenses.
31. Paid interest for May on note payable, $50.

Required

(A) Using the appropriate forms, complete the following:
Define the Account Categories.
Design a suitable Chart of Accounts.
Analyze and record the Transactions on the journal sheet.

(B) Using the computer, do the following:
Create a new company; enter a *code* and the full *company name*.
Select the **INPUT** menu option.
Select the **CATEGORIES** menu option and enter the account categories.
Select the **ACCOUNTS** menu option and enter the accounts.
Select the **TRANSACTIONS** menu option and enter the transactions.
Select the **AUDIT** menu option and view the reports.
If a printer is available, **PRINT** selected reports or a complete package.

The following account balances, in alphabetical order, are from the general ledger of Morgan's Waterproofing Service at January 31, 1993. The firm's accounting year began on January 1. All accounts had normal balances.

Accounts Payable	$ 1,300	Notes Payable	$ 3,000
Accounts Receivable	15,500	Rent Expense	850
Advertising Expense	210	Salaries Expense	4,000
Cash	5,200	Service Fees Earned	12,880
Interest Expense	25	Supplies	4,480
A. Morgan, Capatia l(Jan. 1)	19,870	Supplies Expense	5,125
A. Morgan, Drawing	1,500	Utilities Expense	160

Required

(A) Using the appropriate form, design a <u>Chart of Accounts</u> and appropriate <u>Account Categories</u>.

(B) Enter your <u>Category Definitions</u> and <u>Chart of Accounts</u>.

(C) Enter the January 31 balances as transactions. Use **GJ1** as the journal code and use **BEGIN BALANCE** as the explanation.

(D) Display all reports and complete the financial summary section on the system design form.

Pam Brown owns Art Graphics, a firm providing designs for advertisers, market analysts, and others. On July 1, 1993, her general ledger showed the following normal account balances:

Cash	$ 9,500	Notes Payable	$ 4,000
Accounts Receivable	8,200	Accounts Payable	1,800
		P. Brown, Capital	11,900
	------------		------------
	$ 17,700		$ 17,700
	========		========

The following transactions occurred in July:

July

2 Paid July rent, $580.

2 Collected $6,500 on account from customers.

5 Paid $2,000 installment due on the $4,000 noninterest-bearing note payable to a relative.

9 Billed customers for design services rendered on account, $14,750.

12 Rendered design services and collected from cash customers, $950.

15 Paid $1,200 to creditors on account.

18 Collected $10,800 on account from customers.

21 Paid a delivery service for delivery of graphics to commercial firms, $280.

30 Paid July salaries, $3,200

30 Received invoice for July advertising expense, to be paid in August, $500.

31 Paid cost of utilities for July, $190.

31 Brown withdrew $700 for personal use.

31 Received invoice for supplies used in July, to be paid in August, $2,760.

31 Purchased computer for $5,000 cash to be used in the business starting next month.

Required

(A)   Design a <u>Chart of Accounts</u>. Leave room in your numbering system for future expansion. Define the <u>Account Categories</u>.

(B)   Enter the account categories and chart of accounts.

(C)   Enter the July 1 balances and prepare an opening trial balance. Use **GJ1**.

(D)   Prepare the journal entries for the July transactions.

(E)   Enter the July transactions and prepare financial reports. Use **GJ2**.

Ladd Roofing Service

Mark Ladd opened Ladd Roofing Service on April 1, 1993. Transactions for April are as follows:

Apr. 1 Ladd contributed $9,000 of his personal funds to begin the business.
    2 Purchased a used truck for $5,100 cash.
    2 Purchased ladders and other equipment for a total of $2,800; paid $1,000 cash, with the balance due in 30 days.
    3 Paid three-year premium on liability insurance, $2,700.
    5 Purchased supplies on account, $1,300.
    5 Received an advance payment of $1,600 from a customer for roof repair work to be done during April and May.
  12 Billed customers for roofing services, $3,500.
  18 Collected $2,900 on account from customers.
  29 Paid bill for truck fuel used in April, $60.
  30 Paid April newspaper advertising, $80.
  30 Paid assistants' wages, $2,000.
  30 Billed customers for roofing services, $3,000.

Required

(A)   Design and establish an accounting computer system for Ladd Roofing Service. Provide for accounts needed in the future.

(B)   Prepare and enter the April transactions. Use **J1** as the journal code.

(C)   Produce the financial reports *before* any adjustments.

(D)   Prepare and enter adjustments based on the following:
Insurance Expense. Supplies on hand on April 30 amounted to $400. Depreciation for April was $120 on the truck and $30 on the equipment. One-fourth of the roofing fee received in advance was earned by April 30. Post the adjusting entries.

(E)   Produce the financial reports *after* the adjustments are entered.

Dole Carpet Cleaners

3-29

Dole Carpet Cleaners ended its first month of operations on June 30, 1993. Monthly financial statements will be prepared. The unadjusted account balances are as follows:

Dole Carpet Cleaners
Trial Balance
June 30, 1993

Acct	Description	Debit	Credit
	Cash	980	
	Accounts Receivable	450	
	Prepaid Rent	2,700	
	Supplies	1,900	
	Equipment	4,200	
	Accounts Payable		$ 530
	T. Dole, Capital		7,000
	T. Dole, Drawing	200	
	Service Fees Earned		3,850
	Wages Expense	950	
		$ 11,380	$ 11,380

The following information is also available:

(1) The balance in Prepaid Rent was the amount paid on June 1 for the first four months' rent.
(2) Supplies on hand at June 30 were $740.
(3) The equipment, purchased June 1, has an estimated life of five years.
(4) Unpaid wages at June 30 were $180.
(5) Utility services used during June were estimated at $200. A bill is expected early in July.
(6) Fees earned for services performed but not yet billed on June 30 were $350. The firm uses the account Fees Receivable to reflect amounts due but not yet billed.

Required

Prepare adjusted financial reports. Use a new journal for the adjustments.

Wellness Catering Service

The Wellness Catering Service had the following transactions in July 1993, its first month of operations:

July 1 Kelly Foster contributed $10,000 of personal funds to the business.
1 Purchased the following items for cash from a catering firm that was going out of business (make a compound entry): delivery van, $3,600; equipment, $2,160; and supplies, $1,500.
2 Paid premium on a one-year liability insurance policy, $960.
2 Entered in a contract with a local service club to cater weekly luncheon meetings for one year at a fee of $600 per month. Received six months' fees in advance.
3 Paid rent for July, August, and September, $1,950.
12 Paid employees two weeks' wages (five-day week), $1,400.
15 Billed customers for services rendered, $3,500.
18 Purchased supplies on account, $2,200.
26 Paid employees two weeks' wages, $1,400.
30 Paid July bill for gas, oil, and repairs on delivery van, $570.
30 Collected $2,900 from customers on account.
31 Billed customers for services rendered, $3,800.
31 Kelly withdrew $1,000 for personal use.

Required

Kelly Foster has agreed to try your accounting services for the month of July. Design a system for Wellness Catering Service and process the above transactions. Prepare the *preliminary* financial reports to present to Kelly.

While reviewing the preliminary reports, you have determined that the following items should be reflected in the final report for July.

> Supplies on hand, $1,200
> Accrued wages, $420
> Estimated life of delivery van, three years
> Estimated life of equipment, six years
> Adjusting entries for insurance, rent, and catering fees

Prepare and enter the final adjusting entries using a second journal for the adjustments. Prepare the *final* financial reports.

Keith Howe, Tax Consultant

Keith Howe, tax consultant, began business on December 1, 1993. December transactions were as follows:

Dec. 1 Howe invested $15,000 in the business.
2 Paid rent for December to Star Realty, $800.
2 Purchased various supplies on account, $720.
3 Purchased $7,500 of office equipment, paying $3,700 down with the balance due in 30 days.
8 Paid $720 on account for supplies purchased December 2.
14 Paid assistant's wages for two weeks, $600.
20 Performed consulting services for cash, $2,000.
28 Paid assistant's wages for two weeks, $600.
30 Billed customers for December consulting services, $4,800.
31 Howe withdrew $1,200 from the business.

OPEN THE FOLLOWING LEDGER ACCOUNTS, USING THE ACCOUNT NUMBERS SHOWN:

11 CASH	21 ACCTS PAYABLE	41 CONSULTING REVENUE
12 ACCTS RECEIVABLE	22 WAGES PAYABLE	51 SUPPLIES EXPENSE
13 FEES RECEIVABLE	31 K. HOWE, CAPITAL	52 WAGES EXPENSE
14 SUPPLIES	32 K. HOWE, DRAWING	53 RENT EXPENSE
15 OFFICE EQUIPMENT	33 INCOME SUMMARY	54 DEPR EXPENSE
16 ACCUM DEPR - EQUIP		

Required

(A) Prepare preliminary financial reports.

(B) Prepare the final financial reports.

The following information is available for year-end adjustments. Use a second journal for the adjustments.

(1) Supplies on hand at December 31 is $470.
(2) Accrued Wages Payable at December 31 is $180.
(3) Depreciation for December is $80.
(4) Howe has spent 20 hours on an involved tax fraud case during December. When completed in January, his work will be billed at $50 per hour.
(Note: The firm uses the account Fees Receivable to reflect amounts earned but not yet billed.)

The unadjusted trial balance of Wong Distributors on December 31, 1993, is shown below; the periodic inventory system has been used.

Wong Distributors
Trial Balance
December 31, 1993

ACCT	ACCOUNT DESCRIPTION	DEBIT	CREDIT
1100	Cash	$ 15,200	
1200	Account Receivable	80,200	
1300	Inventory	138,000	
1400	Prepaid Insurance	7,200	
1410	Supplies	6,400	
1600	Delivery Equipment	80,000	
1650	Accum Depreciation		$ 19,000
2010	Accounts Payable		69,600
3000	T. Wong, Capital		168,000
3100	T. Wong, Drawing	26,000	
4100	Sales		812,000
4200	Sales Returns & Allow	11,600	
4210	Sales Discounts	14,600	
5000	Beginning Inventory	0	
5100	Purchases	522,000	
5110	Purchases Returns		5,200
5200	Purchases Discounts		10,200
5210	Transportation-In	12,800	
5300	Ending Inventory		0
6100	Salaries Expense	108,000	
6200	Rent Expense	40,000	
6300	Gas/Repairs Expense	18,400	
6400	Utilities Expense	3,600	
		$ 1,084,000	$ 1,084,000

Continued

Wong Distributors

The following information is available at December 31, 1993:

(1) Prepaid Insurance at December 31 is $2,400.
(2) Supplies at December 31 amount to $4,200.
(3) Depreciation on the delivery equipment is 20% per year.
(4) At December 31, the company owes its employees $1,200 in salaries.
(5) At December 31, the company has not recorded a utility bill for $280. Use a Utilities Payable account.
(6) Inventory at December 31 is $144,000.

Required

(A) Define and enter the account categories. For the Operating Costs category, include accounts 5000 to 5999. The total of this category will represent the cost of goods sold.

(B) Enter the chart of accounts.

(C) Enter the beginning balances as transactions. Use a journal code and a date that will indicate the nature of the balances.

(D) Analyze, record, and enter the December 31 adjustments in a new journal.

Most manual procedures to adjust the Inventory account will not work with a computer system. In order for the computer to calculate the cost Of goods sold, we must explicitly direct the balances to accounts that can be used in this calculation. Also, these accounts must be in the category for cost of goods sold.

When adjusting the inventory account, three accounts should be used.

ACCT 1300 Inventory (balance sheet)
ACCT 5000 Beginning Inventory (income statement)
ACCT 5300 Ending Inventory (income statement)

Two entries are recommended. *First*, transfer the beginning balance from account 1300 to account 5000 with a debit to account 5000 and a credit to account 1300. At this point, account 1300 will have a zero balance. You have transferred the beginning inventory balance from the balance sheet to the income statement. *Second*, enter the ending balance as a debit to account 1300 and a credit to account 5300.

Lincoln Distributors has the following accounts and balances as of January 1.

ACCT	Description	Amount	ACCT	Description
110	Cash	$ 6,000	410	Sales
120A	Acct Rec--Cooper Company	650	420	Sales Returns
120B	Acct Rec--Lyons, Inc.	400	430	Sales Discounts
120C	Acct Rec--Thomas Company	900	440	Misc Income
120D	Acct Rec--White Company	300		
140	Inventory	30,000		
150	Store Supplies	800	510	Purchases
160	Office Supplies	700	520	Purchases Returns
170	Equipment	24,000	530	Purchases Discounts
180	Accum Depreciation	(6,000)	540	Transportation In
210A	Acct Pay--Davis Company	(450)		
210B	Acct Pay--Lenz Suppliers	(950)	610	Rent Expense
210C	Acct Pay--Sprague, Inc.	(700)	620	Salaries Expense
310	R. Lincoln, Capital	(55,650)	630	Transportation Out
320	R. Lincoln, Drawing		640	Misc Expense

Lincoln Distributors, which sells on terms of 2/10, n/30 and uses the periodic inventory system, had the following transactions during January 1993.

Cash Receipts Journal (CRJ)

DATE	ACCT	AMOUNT	DESCRIPTION
01/	8	$ 400.00C	From Lyons, Inc. on account
		8.00	Sales discount taken by Lyons, Inc.
	8	900.00C	From Thomas Company on account
	8	300.00C	From White Company on account
		6.00	Sales discount taken by White Company
	16	650.00C	From Cooper Company on account
	18	620.00C	From Lyons, Inc. on account
	31	250.00C	Cash sale of merchandise
	31	405.00C	Misc. income for use of billboard
		$3,511.00	January cash receipts

C = Credit amount

Continued

Lincoln Distributors

Cash Disbursements Journal (CDJ)

DATE	ACCT	AMOUNT	CK#	DESCRIPTION
01/	1	$ 600.00	200	January rent
	2	700.00	201	Paid Sprague, Inc. full amount owed
		14.00C		Less 2% discount on Sprague, Inc. payment
	3	450.00	202	Paid Davis Company
	3	950.00	203	Paid Lenz Suppliers
	10	55.00	204	Freight to Ruan Freight (freight out)
	15	40.00	205	Freight to Arrow Transport (freight In)
	15	900.00	206	Salary for L. Voss
	15	900.00	207	Salary for C. Downs
	21	900.00	208	Paid Davis Co. for Jan. 14 purchase
		9.00C		Less purchase discount on Davis purchase
	22	50.00	209	Paid misc. expenses
	24	500.00	210	Check to R. Linclon for a personal draw
		$6,013.00C		January cash disbursements

Sales Journal (SJ)

DATE	ACCT	AMOUNT	INVOICE	DESCRIPTION
01/	7	$ 620.00	No.470	Lyons, Inc.
	9	780.00	No.471	Thomas Company
	30	1,400.00	No.472	White Company
		$2,800.00C		January credit sales

Purchase Journal (PJ)

DATE	ACCT	AMOUNT	Description
01/	14	$ 900.00	Merchandise
		900.00C	Davis Company on account
	18	120.00	Store supplies
		600.00	Equipment
		70.00	Office supplies
		790.00C	Lenz Suppliers on account
	28	1,500.00	Merchandise
		1,500.00C	Sprague, Inc. on account

C = Credit amount

Continued

Lincoln Distributors

General Journal (GJ)

DATE	ACCT	AMOUNT	DESCRIPTION
10/11		180.00	Sales returns
		180.00C	Thomas Company credit memo
29		300.00	Sprague, Inc. goods returned
		300.00C	Purchase return

C= Credit amount

Required

(A) Establish a system for Lincoln and enter the beginning balances.

(B) Enter the account code directly in the journal or prepare a transaction journal form for the special journals. Use the customer's/vendor's account code when appropriate.

In practice, it is better to minimize the number of times that data are copied from one form to another. For example, the cash disbursements journal usually consists of the numeric copy of the check, bound together with a cover sheet indicating the cash total for the period. The account code is entered directly on each check copy. Computer input then consists of entering each check with related data such as check number, account code, and amount. After all checks have been entered, the total of all cash paid is entered as one amount with a credit to the cash account.

The general ledger cash account then shows only the totals for the period. The audit trail for cash flows from the Cash account to the cash journals.

(C) Enter each journal using a journal code that is appropriate. The letter C has been used in the journal to indicate a credit amount.

(D) Prepare the unadjusted reports as of January 31.

Rindt Distributors

6-28

The post-closing trial balance at December 31, 1992, for Rindt Distributors is given below:

Rindt Distributors
Post-Closing Trial Balance
December 31, 1992

	DEBIT	CREDIT
Cash	$ 12,200	
Account Receivable	22,000	
Inventory	66,300	
Office Supplies	740	
Store Supplies	410	
Office Equipment	13,000	
Accum Depreciation		$ 4,800
Accounts Payable		31,200
L. Rindt, Capital		78,650
	$ 114,650	$ 114,650

Rindt maintains special journals for cash receipts, cash payments, purchases, and sales. You have been requested to set up a computer system for the new year, beginning with the month of January. Although Rindt would like you to review the detail of each journal, you are asked to computerize only the summary of the special journals (see following page).

Required

(A) Design a computer system and process the beginning trial balance.

(B) Using the summarized journals, enter the January transactions. Notice that credit amounts are followed by the letter **C**.

(C) Prepare the January 31, 1993, unadjusted reports.

Continued

Rindt Distributors

At the end of January, 1993, the totals of the firm's special journals, before posting, are as follows:

Sales Journal (SJ)

Accounts Receivable	$98,900
Sales	98,900.C

Purchase Journal (PJ)

Accounts Payable	$87,800.C
Purchases	82,300
Office Supplies	600
Store Supplies	900
Office Equipment	4,000

Cash Receipts Journal (CRJ)

Cash	95,830
Sales Discounts	1,420
Accounts Receivable	77,400.C
Sales	11,850.C
L. Rindt, Capital	8,000.C

Cash Disbursements Journal (CDJ)

Cash	80,240.C
Purchases Discounts	960.C
Accounts Payable	75,200
Rent Expense	1,900
Advertising Expense	900
Salaries Expense	3,200

C = Credit Amount

SoftSales - Part 1

Chris Davis purchased a microcomputer about three years ago. It was love at first sight or, in this case, you might say at first byte. Chris has quite a list of accomplishments with his computer. He has become an accomplished programmer in Pascal, Basic, and Assembly Language.

Chris has also been in demand as a free-lance programmer, earning more than enough to totally support his education. As a matter of fact, his programming effort has resulted in more business than he can handle. It seems that Chris has to make a decision regarding his education. With all of his business activity, he doubts whether he can continue to pursue his degree in computer science.

It seems that you have a similiar problem about continuing your degree but for completely different reasons. Your income does not provide enough support for your education. Chris is a good friend of yours. As you discuss your situations, it occurs to both of you that you can help each other.

Chris agrees to turn all of the accounting, office management, and other business related activities over to you while he concentrates on programming. He would like to call his company SoftSales and will sign all checks and other legal documents. You are requested to find and negotiate suitable office space as well as handle all aspects of the new business. Although you have never set up a business, a little research shows that you should do the following:

File an application for a business license.
Request federal and state identification numbers.
Open a bank account with <u>City Bank</u>.

Chris is depending on you to design and maintain an accounting system that will provide current information relative to cash and other important activities. You have explained that your computer system will provide immediate information for any aspect of the business with two or three keystrokes at any time.

You have promised Chris that accounting information will be available for him to review at any time. You both agree that the accounting records will be completely reviewed and adjusted at the end of each calendar quarter.

You have defined the account categories and chart of accounts as shown on the following page. Enter these into the computer system.

The following activity occured during the first quarter of 1993. Analyze, record, and add these transactions to the SoftSales data base.

DATE T R A N S A C T I O N D E S C R I P T I O N

1/3   Chris signed a contract with Active Video, Inc. for custom programming on an hourly basis at $55 per hour. This contract is in the name of SoftSales and is to extend over a three-month period.

1/4   To open the bank account with City Bank and to provide initial operating funds, Chris invests $3,000 in the company.

1/4   You have located office space and have negotiated a one-year lease for SoftSales. Issued Check 101 for $1,800 to Landmark Properties for six months' rent at $300 per month.

1/6   Issued Check 102 for $380 to Peninsula Office for supplies.

1/20   Issued Invoice 501 to Active Video, Inc. for 35 hours of programming. Set up a separate account for Active Video.

1/31   Issued Check 103 for $750 to yourself for January services.

1/31   Record adjustments for January rent and supplies used.
       You estimate supplies on hand to be $150.

After reviewing the cash position, Chris requests a complete accounting of all activity to date. Chris does not understand why there is a difference between the cash balance of $70 and the reported net income of $645. Please prepare an explanation.

SoftSales - Category Definitions

BALANCE SHEET	BEG#	END#	INCOME STATEMENT	BEG#	END#
Current Assets	1000	1799	Operating Revenues	4000	4899
Long-Term Assets	1800	1899	Other Revenues	4900	4999
Other Assets	1900	1999	Operating Costs	5000	5999
Current Liabilities	2000	2789	Operating Expenses	6000	6899
Long-Term Liabilities	2800	2999	Other Expenses	6900	6999
Owner Equity	3000	3999			

SoftSales - Chart of Accounts

BALANCE SHEET

ACCT	DESCRIPTION
1100	CASH--CITY BANK
1210	AR--ACTIVE VIDEO
1220	AR--
1230	AR--
1300	INVENTORY
1410	SUPPLIES ON HAND
1510	PREPAID RENT
1810	OFFICE FURNITURE
1819	ACCUM DEPR FURNITURE
1820	COMPUTER EQUIPMENT
1829	ACCUM COMPUTER EQUIP
2200	AP--GENERAL
2210	AP--SAMPSON COMPANY
2220	AP--
2230	AP--
2400	NOTE PAY--W. DAVIS
3100	C. DAVIS, CAPITAL
3200	C. DAVIS, DRAWING

INCOME STATEMENT

ACCT	DESCRIPTION
4000	PROGRAMMING FEES
4100	SALES--PROGRAMS
4190	SALES RETURNS
5100	BEGINNING INVENTORY
5200	PURCHASES
5290	PURCHASES RETURNS
5900	ENDING INVENTORY
6100	SALARY EXPENSE
6200	RENT EXPENSE
6300	SUPPLIES EXPENSE
6310	TELEPHONE EXPENSE
6810	DEPR EXP--FURNITURE
6820	DEPR EXP--COMPUTERS

Also, Chris is planning to buy a computer and office furniture, totaling about $6,500. He will need reports for a lender. Prepare a complete report package as of the end of January.

February transactions are as follows:

2/3   Purchased office furniture on account for $2,415 from Sampson Furniture Company. Estimated life to be five years.

2/5   Chris arranged for SoftSales to borrow $4,800 from his father. Chris signed an interest-free note for two years with equal payments of $600 to be made at the beginning of each calendar quarter starting April 1, 1987. Deposited the cash received.

2/6   Paid cash for an IBM PC microcomputer in the amount of $4,032 to be used for software development. The purchase price includes a printer and a clock/calendar card with 356k of RAM disk. Estimated life to be three years. Issued Check 104.

2/15 Collected the full amount billed to Active Video on Invoice 501.

2/20 Issued Check 105 to Chris for a personal draw of $850.

2/25 Issued Invoice 502 to Active Video for 48 hours of programming.

2/28 Issued Check 106 for $750 to yourself for February services.

2/28 Received February telephone bill from Pacific Bell for $85. This is to be paid by March 15th.

Do not prepare any adjusting entries at the end of February. The records will be adjusted next month at the end of the quarter. March transactions are as follows:

3/2   Chris asks you to pay $1,000 to Sampson Furniture Company on account only if there is enough cash to cover this and the phone bill which is due by March 15. Chris expects to receive payment from Active Video by March 20. This can be used to pay your salary by the end of the month. If there is not enough cash, then pay $500 to Sampson. Use Check 107 for the payment.

3/10 Purchased supplies on account from Peninsula Office for $250.

3/15 Paid February telephone bill using Check 108.

3/20   Received full payment from Active Video for Invoice 502.

3/21   Billed Active Video for 60 hours of programming. Use Invoice 503.

3/22   Issued Check 109 to Chris for a personal draw of $1,300.

3/30   Issued Check 110 for your salary of $750.

PREPARE AND RECORD MARCH 31 ADJUSTMENTS

(1)   Supplies on hand amount to $130.
(2)   Adjust for office rent (February and March).
(3)   Depreciation on office furniture. No salvage value.
(4)   Depreciation on IBM PC microcomputer. No salvage value.
(5)   March telephone bill is $145.

PREPARE THE ADJUSTED FINANCIAL REPORTS AND RECORD BELOW THE SELECTED AMOUNTS.

NET INCOME $_____   ASSETS $_____

TOTAL REVENUE $_____   LIABILITIES $_____

PROFIT MARGIN _____% OWNER EQUITY $_____

SoftSales - Part 2

Chris has found a supplier of general-purpose inventory control programs. Because most companies have their own unique inventory problems, general programs do not provide a complete answer. Chris has discovered that he can modify these general programs for particular industries and market them directly to computer distributors.

Chris has arranged to buy these programs from Software Solutions and he has located two distributors that are very interested in the modified programs. Software Solutions will extend partial credit but requires part of the purchase price to be paid in cash with delivery of each order. You have decided to use the periodic method in accounting for the inventory. All programs purchased will be charged to the Purchase account.

Student Note

All transactions for the first quarter were given in narrative form and were recorded as a general journal entry with a debit and a credit for each transaction. In practice, this *is not* the case. In practice, most entries are originated and supported by source documents that are coded directly and grouped together, providing the basis for entry into the transaction database.

Examples of source documents are the following:

Buying   **Purchase Invoices, Checks, Debit Memos**

Selling   **Sales Invoices, Deposit Slips, Credit Memos**

In a *manual accounting system*, the source document detail is recorded in *special journals*. Each journal has a different format and has special rules for posting to the general ledger and the subsidiary ledgers. Data are summarized within the special journal before posting. This reduces the number of postings but severly limits the information available in the Ledger. No source document reference numbers are available, and the amounts posted are usually summary amounts, which do not provide a ready means of analysis.

In a *computer accounting system*, the source documents are often entered *directly* into the database. In this case, the source document is the journal. However, before documents can be entered, they must be prepared for entry. For example, *checks* often have three parts: the original to be sent for payment, a numeric copy, and an alpha copy. The alpha copy could be filed by vendor and the numeric copy prepared for data entry into the computer system.

The *numeric* copies for a month are grouped together and totaled. Each check is coded directly for the account to be *debited*. If the amount owed has already been recorded as a liability, then the vendor's account will be debited; otherwise, the appropriate account will be debited. After the debits for all checks have been entered, the cash account must be *credited* for the total of the cash paid for the month. It is advisable to record the check number and payee as part of the explanation for each debit. This will provide a direct *audit trail* from any ledger account to the source document.

Although *checks* are coded only with the account debited, some source documents need both a debit and a credit coded on each document. For example, purchase invoices will be coded with a *debit* for what is purchased and a *credit* to the vendors account. SalesInvoices will be coded with a *debit* to the customers account and a *credit* to the appropriate revenue account.

The activity for the second quarter is grouped by source documents. Consider each line item to be the source document, enter the appropriate account code next to the date in the space provided, and indicate whether it is a debit or a credit. Each Purchase Invoice and Sales Invoice will need to be double coded (as both a debit and a credit). Use the column next to the date, which is titled <u>ACCT/ACCT</u>. Use the first account for the debit and the second account for the credit. Entering each of these documents into the database will require two line entries.

Enter all activity for each month and review the reports. At the end of the second quarter, June 30, the books will be adjusted and reports prepared.

PJ - PURCHASES ON ACCOUNT (Purchase Invoices)

DATE	ACCT/ACCT	AMOUNT	P.O.#	DESCRIPTION
4/5		$ 2,200.00	125	Software Solutions--programs/net 30
5/6		$ 4,340.00	126	Software Solutions--programs/net 30
6/15		$ 6,720.00	127	Software Solutions--programs/net 30

CP - CASH PAYMENTS (Checks Paid)

DATE	ACCT	AMOUNT	CK#	DESCRIPTION
4/2		$ 600.00	111	W. Davis--First quarterly payment
4/5		1,900.00	112	Software Solutions-purchases
4/8		145.00	113	Pacific Bell--March bill
4/15		1,200.00	114	Sampson Furniture--on account
4/30		750.00	115	*your name*--April salary
4/30				April cash payments
5/5		$ 2,200.00	116	Software Solutions--on account
5/6		1,860.00	117	Software Solutions--purchases
5/15		170.00	118	Pacific Bell--April bill
5/24		680.00	119	Penn Office--supplies
5/24		215.00	120	Sampson Furniture--paid in full
5/31		1,150.00	121	*your name*--May salary
5/31				May cash payments
6/8		$ 4,340.00	122	Software Solutions--on account
6/15		160.00	123	Pacific Bell--May bill
6/15		1,680.00	124	Software Solutions--purchases
6/20		350.00	125	Data Store--supplies
6/30		1,150.00	126	*your name*--June salary
6/30				June cash payments

SJ - SALES ON ACCOUNT   (Sales Invoices)

DATE	ACCT/ACCT	AMOUNT	INV#	DESCRIPTION
4/20		$ 1,200.00	504	Computer Resources--programs
4/22		1,600.00	505	Instant Info, Inc.--programs
4/23		5,200.00	506	Active Video--80 hrs/$65
5/6		$ 3,200.00	507	Computer Resources--programs
5/10		1,950.00	508	Instant Info, Inc.--programs
5/25		6,500.00	509	Active Video--100 hrs/$65
6/12		$ 3,100.00	510	Instant Info, Inc.--programs
6/15		4,525.00	511	Computer Resources--programs
6/24		4,875.00	512	Active Video--75 hrs/$65

CR - CASH RECEIPTS (Deposits Made)

DATE	ACCT	AMOUNT	DESCRIPTION
4/7		$ 2,500.00	C. Davis, investment
4/7		3,300.00	Active Video--on account
4/30			April cash receipts
5/25		$ 600.00	Computer Resources--on account
5/27		1,600.00	Instant Info, Inc.--paid Inv#505
5/27		5,200.00	Active Video--on account
5/31			May cash receipts
6/20		$ 6,500.00	Active Video--on account
6/23		1,750.00	Computer Resources--on account
6/26		1,950.00	Instant Info, Inc.--paid Inv#508
6/30			June cash receipts

GJ - GENERAL JOURNAL (Other Transactions)

5/10   Issued a credit memo to Computer Resources for programs returned in the amount of $450.

6/12   Issued a debit memo to Software Solutions for $620 for defective disks which were returned.

PREPARE AND RECORD THE JUNE 30 ADJUSTMENTS

(1)   Supplies on hand amount to about $240.

(2)   Office rent for the second quarter.

(3)   Depreciation on the office furniture and the computer equipment.

(4)   June telephone bill is $172.

(5)   Inventory of programs as of June 30 is $3,860.

PREPARE THE SECOND QUARTER ADJUSTED FINANCIAL REPORTS AND COMPLETE THE ANALYSIS BELOW AS OF JUNE 30, 1990:

NET INCOME $_____   ASSETS $_____

TOTAL REVENUE $_____   LIABILITIES $_____

PROFIT MARGIN _____%   OWNER EQUITY $_____

RETURN ON ASSETS _____%

RETURN ON EQUITY _____%

PART TWO

■

The Electronic Spreadsheet

The Electronic Spreadsheet

Manual Worksheet   Electronic Worksheet

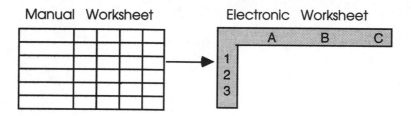

SOLVE the problem manually

PROGRAM the relationships

CREATE the electronic worksheet

ANALYZE your solutions

Spreadsheet Perspectives

Very Broad User Base

The spreadsheet is the most widely used computer applications program. For this to be true, the spreadsheet would have to provide practical solutions for a wide range of real problems. This is exactly why the spreadsheet is so popular: it provides solutions for many users over a very broad base. Although most spreadsheet users are concerned with business or financial applications, many scientists, engineers, and others use the spreadsheet to analyze and solve many of their problems.

Common Characteristics of Spreadsheet Applications

At first, there may seem to be little in common over the range of spreadsheet applications. However, a closer inspection will reveal some common characteristics of the many problems that can be solved using the spreadsheet. Most of the problems can be described by stating *relationships* among the data elements that are available for analysis. These relationships are expressed in *formulas*. Formulas are then used to link the spreadsheet cells together into an overall structure.

Spreadsheets - A Method of Programming

Although some spreadsheet users may not recognize it, the process of expressing and declaring relationships is actually a method of programming. It is quite different from writing a *procedural program* of well-defined steps that must be executed in a particular sequence. The spreadsheet is a *declarative program* that defines the relationships between data elements. Some problems are easier to solve using the procedural approach, and others are much easier to solve using the declarative approach.

Spreadsheets - Declarative Programs

Spreadsheets provide the first effective environment for writing and running declarative programs. Declarative programming is a process of defining relationships between the data elements of a given problem.

First, an understanding of the problem is required. Without a firm understanding of the problem, it is difficult, if not impossible, to express the relationships.

Second, the various elements are organized according to their dependency level. Some data elements are independent of the values of any of the other elements, but some elements are not. The independent elements can be treated as inputs to the problem; the dependent elements can be shown as calculated outputs.

Third, relationships are declared for all the dependent elements. These relationships are expressed as formulas. Together, the formulas and independent inputs make up the total program.

Spreadsheet Organization

Spreadsheet Structure

The following spreadsheet consists of two columns and eight rows. **Columns** are identified by the letters A and B across the top; **rows** are identified by the numbers 1 through 8 down the left side. The intersection of each row and column is called a *cell*. With two columns and eight rows, this spreadsheet contains 16 cells. Each cell has a specific address consisting of the column letter and the row number of the cell's location. For example, cell B4 contains the number 120,000, and cell A4 contains the label "Revenue."

	A	B
1	Preparer's Name:	
2	Spreadsheet Title:	Income Statement
3		JAN
4	Revenue	120,000
5	Expense	78,000
6	Net Income	+B4-B5
7		
8	Profit Percentage	+B6/B4

Independent Inputs

B4	Revenue
B5	Expense

Dependent Outputs

B6	Net Income

Cell Contents

The contents of any cell can contain only one of three possible types of data.

(1) <u>LABELS</u>. Labels are used for descriptive or informative purposes only. For example, all data in column A are descriptive and are not used in calculations.

(2) <u>NUMBERS</u>. Numbers are supplied by the user and are entered directly when processing the spreadsheet. In the example above, two numbers are found in cells B4 and B5. The number in cell B4 represents the revenue amount and the number in cell B5 represents the expense amount. We will refer to these numbers as *independent inputs* or simply as <u>inputs</u>.

(3) FORMULAS. Formulas are programmed instructions designed and entered by the creator of the spreadsheet. These formulas explicitly define the relationships between the numbers or inputs supplied by the user and the calculated outputs produced by the formulas. In our example, two formulas are found in cells B6 and B8. These formulas produce a numeric result. We will refer to the numeric result produced as *dependent outputs* or simply as outputs.

Independent Inputs and Dependent Outputs

The numbers supplied by the user may change each time the spreadsheet is run. The value of these numbers does not depend on any element of the problem. Also, they do not depend on each other for their values. Therefore, the numeric inputs supplied by the user are called independent inputs. Formulas are used to convert the numeric inputs to the desired outputs, which we will call dependent outputs because their value depends on the value of the inputs.

Spreadsheet Operations

Spreadsheet Creators

The main tasks of the creator are spreadsheet design and spreadsheet programming. The *design phase* includes a thorough researching of the problem. What is known and what results are desired? Who will the primary users be? What are the sources of data input? These and similar questions are fundamental to the basic design. The creator then has a basis for the preliminary layout for the spreadsheet. Keeping in mind that there are only three possibilities for each cell--labels, input numbers, and formulas that produce the desired results--the creator then organizes the spreadsheet format.

In the *programming stage*, all expected input from the user must be related to the anticipated outputs to the problem. In other words, relationships between all data elements must be firmly established. These relationships are established using formulas. The formulas will be in the form of explicit instructions for calculating the desired results. In the example, the two formulas in cells B6 and B8 define the relationships between the inputs in cells B4 and B5 and the outputs in cells B6 and B8. Notice that the formulas reside in the same cells as the desired outputs. In programming the outputs, the creator does not give the actual result but rather gives the *procedure* for the calculation of the desired results. Once this concept is understood, it makes sense for the formulas to be placed in the cells where the output results will be found.

Comparison of the Roles of the Creator and the User

As Entered by the Creator

Preparer's Name:	*your name*	
Spreadsheet Title:	Income Statement	
	JAN	
Revenue		
Expense		
Net Income	+B4-B5	
Profit Percentage	+B6/B4	

As Displayed by the User

Preparer's Name:	*your name*	
Spreadsheet Title:	Income Statement	
	JAN	
Revenue	120,000	
Expense	78,000	
Net Income	42,000	
Profit Percentage	35.00%	

Spreadsheet Users

Once the spreadsheet is designed and programmed by the creator, it is ready to be used for its intended purpose, processing data electronically. The user supplies numeric data inputs, which are processed by the formulas programmed by the creator. The numeric results are displayed. These are then analyzed by the user. These results may be used as input to another problem, or they may be used to support decision-making activity.

The power of electronic spreadsheets is demonstrated by changing any of the input values and instantly processing the revised results. What would take minutes or hours to process manually can be accomplished in seconds with the electronic spreadsheet. This power allows the user to experiment with many probable inputs to understand better the effects of the decisions that will be made.

The Problem Solver

The small business computer and spreadsheet application programs have brought computing power directly into the hands of the problem solver. With this power, the problem solver can literally become the spreadsheet designer, programmer, and user. The gap between the problem solver and the data processer or programmer has been eliminated to a large extent. This revolution promises to bring the process of problem solving into better focus for the decision maker. For the accountant, the electronic spreadsheet has far-reaching possibilities that are now being realized.

Lotus 1-2-3 is the software program used in the Electronic Spreadsheet section of the Computer Resource Guide. (For information on the accounting cycle portion of the software, please see Part One of this manual.) Much of the acceptance of the IBM PC microcomputer is due to the popularity of this program. Learning to use Lotus 1-2-3 will greatly enhance your ability to compete in the job market.

You are encouraged to use the Lotus tutorial (part of the Lotus 1-2-3 disk package) if you have never used Lotus before. This manual is not a working substitute for the Lotus 1-2-3 User's Manual.

Please read these instructions completely before you begin. After you read them , complete all of the practice exercises in the order given. These practice exercises are essential to the material that follows. You will then be ready to begin work on the sample problems that follow in Chapter 9.

Requirements

◆ IBM PC, XT, or AT microcomputer with 5 1/4-inch, 360 KB drive and monitor **OR** IBM PS/2 with 3 1/2-inch, 720 KB drive. (This package is available from the publisher in both formats.)
◆ Two double-sided, double-density disk drives for IBM PC; one floppy disk drive for IBM XT or AT.
◆ 256 K RAM of memory.
◆ LOTUS 1-2-3 System Disk, version 1A or 2.
◆ 80-column, parallel printer (if worksheets are to be printed).

Program Execution and General Instructions

(Users of the IBM AT and IBM XT should modify these instructions as needed.)

(A) Insert the **Lotus 1-2-3 System Disk** in DRIVE A and close the disk drive door. Insert the **CRG Disk** in DRIVE B and close the disk drive door.

(B) Boot the system by turning on the power (if not already on) or by pressing the **<Ctrl>** key, the **<Alt>** key, and the **<Del>** key simultaneously.

(C) An on-screen message will ask you to enter the date and time. If you are lucky enough to be using a computer with a built-in clock, this information will not be requested. The date and time are recorded with newly created or modified files. Enter the date in the format MM-DD-YY and press the **<Return>** key. Enter the time in the format HH:MM and press the **<Return>** key. Because the time is less important than the date, you may ignore this request by just pressing the **<Return>** key without entering the time. When the computer is ready, the letter A followed by a greater than sign will appear on the screen, as **A>**.

(D) Type <u>**Lotus**</u> and press the **<Return>** key. After several seconds the **Lotus Access System** screen will appear. Press the **<Return>** key. After a few more seconds the **Copyright** screen will appear. Press any key to continue. Finally, a blank worksheet will appear. You are now ready to create a new worksheet or load an existing worksheet.

(E) Use reasonable care in handling your floppy disks. Do not touch the oblong read/write exposed area. Do not expose the disk to heat or magnetic fields because this could destroy the data.

The <u>1-2-3</u> Worksheet Window

Your view of the <u>1-2-3</u> worksheet is limited to a very small part of the total area. The worksheet window, which is displayed on the computer monitor and shown below, contains some very important information that will help you control the worksheet activity. Understanding and controlling the worksheet activity are main learning objectives.

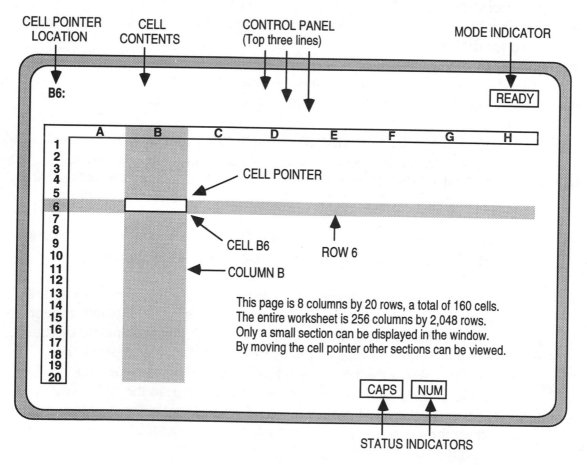

You will control the worksheet window activity by your skillful use of the keyboard. As you send instructions to the 1-2-3 program, it will interpret your instructions according to its built-in program. 1-2-3 will then communicate its understanding of your instructions by displaying certain activity in the worksheet window. If you watch the worksheet window as you press the keyboard keys, you will quickly learn many of 1-2-3's secrets. Understanding the following window components will be essential in beginning to understand the activity of 1-2-3.

Window Components

Control Panel - The three lines across the top of the window.

First Line: This line contains the cell's address and contents.

Second Line: This line displays the cell contents as you type it. This line also displays the command menu items and prompts.

Third Line: This line displays messages as well as submenus.

Columns - The letters across the top of the worksheet labeled A through IV.

Rows - The numbers down the left side of the worksheet from 1 through 2,048.

Cells - Rectangular boxes formed by the intersection of a row and column.

Cell Pointer - The highlighted area that marks the active cell, the "pointer."

Mode Indicator - The highlighted box in the top right corner that indicates the current mode of operation. 1-2-3 will use this to tell you what it thinks you are doing. The mode can change quickly, so keep an eye on this to learn the various types of activity allowed by 1-2-3. You can think of this as the "mood" indicator of 1-2-3. The mood of 1-2-3 determines what you can do, but you are able to control what the mood will be.

Status Indicators - The bottom box that shows which keys have been activated, such as the Caps Lock key or the Number Lock key.

The Keyboard

You control the worksheet window activity with the keyboard. An understanding of the keys and the related activity will evolve as you practice using 1-2-3. The keyboard contains various types of keys: typewriter keys, pointer movement keys, data correction/edit keys, function keys, and special keys.

The center section of the keyboard contains keys that act like a typewriter. The letters are in the usual places, and the numbers are on the top row. Using the **<Shift>** key (the hollow up arrow on either side) will give you a capital letter or the special characters on the number keys at the top. In addition to the normal typewriter keys, you will find many keys that have special uses. These keys are shown in the keyboard diagram below and are briefly described in the section that follows. As you become proficient in the use of 1-2-3, these keys and their uses will play an important role.

IBM PC Keyboard Layout

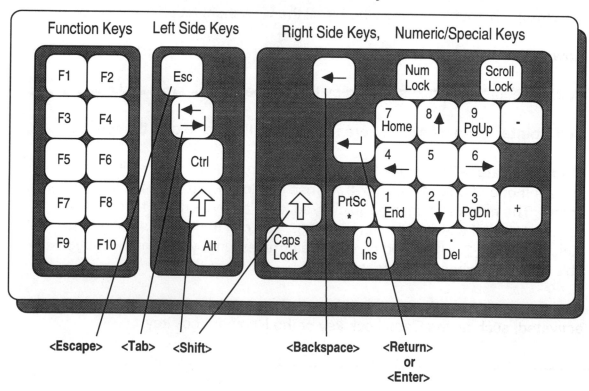

Data Entry/Correction Keys

<Return>	Complete a cell entry or a command prompt, same as Enter (left-pointing bent arrow key to the left of the **<Home>** key)
<Shift>	Uppercase letters, special characters (Hollow, upward arrows on either side)
<Escape>	Back up one step, cancel current entry, return to Ready mode
<Backspace>	Move the cursor back one character while erasing (left-pointing arrow key, above the **<Return>** key)
<F2>	Switch to edit mode for the active cell (F2 function key)
<Del>	In edit mode, delete character at cursor position

Pointer-Movement Keys

<Up>	Move pointer one cell up (up arrow key)
<Down>	Move pointer one cell down (down arrow key)
<Right>	Move pointer one cell right (right arrow key)
<Left>	Move pointer one cell left (left arrow key)
<Home>	Go to top (cell A1) of worksheet
<End>	Use with other pointer keys
<PgUp>	Flip one page up
<PgDn>	Flip one page down
<Tab>	Flip one page right (double arrow key)
<Shift><Tab>	Flip one page left (double arrow key)

Special Keys

<Shift><PrtSc>	Makes an exact printed copy of the display screen
<CapsLock>	Toggle switch: changes letter case, upper-lower
<NumLock>	Toggle switch: changes pointer keys to numeric pad
<ScrollLock>	Toggle switch: changes pointer movement keys
<Alt>	Use with letter keys for macro execution
<Ctrl>	Control key for special functions
<Ctrl><Alt><Del>	Reboot the system, referred to as a "warm boot"

Function Keys

<F1>	**Help**	Display help screen
<F2>	**Edit**	Switch to edit mode for the active cell
<F3>	**Name**	In point mode, display range names
<F4>	**Absolute**	In point mode, make cell an absolute reference
<F5>	**Go To**	Move pointer to a particular cell
<F6>	**Window**	Move pointer to the other split screen
<F7>	**Query**	Repeat data query operation
<F8>	**Table**	Repeat data table operation
<F9>	**Calculate**	Recalculate the worksheet
<F10>	**Graph**	Draw most recently specified graph

NOTE: Use the help screens.

If the Lotus 1-2-3 System Disk is still in Drive A, pressing the **<F1>** help key will display help screens. You will find the screens to be full of helpful information, possibly more that you can absorb at any one time. As you become more experienced, this information will become more meaningful. When you want to return to the workshee,t simply press the **<Escape>** key, and you will return to where you were.

The help screens are "context sensitive," which means that the information shown will depend on what you are doing at the time you press the help key. 1-2-3 knows where you are when you request help and provides appropriate information. Used wisely, this feature will give you an opportunity to learn 1-2-3's secrets quickly .

IMPORTANT: Do the practice exercises.

The following sections include practice exercises that are very important in using 1-2-3. Please read all of the material before using the computer. This will give you an idea of 1-2-3's basic operations. Then, using the computer, complete all of the practice exercises that are marked with a check (✓). These exercises will prepare you for the sample problems in Chapter 9.

Moving around the Worksheet

The most basic worksheet activity involves moving from one cell to another and entering labels and values. The pointer movement keys will allow you to reach your destination easily. The arrow keys will move the pointer one cell at a time as shown in the diagram.

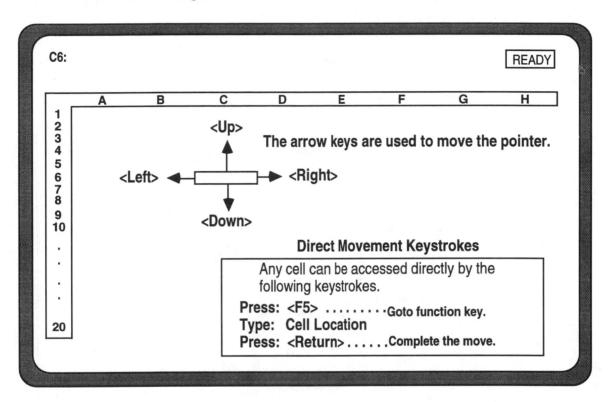

Practice pointer key movement.

✓ Using the arrow keys, move the pointer a few times. Notice that 1-2-3 beeps each time you hit the top or left edge of the worksheet. Als, notice that the cell address in the first line of the control panel changes to correspond with the position of the pointer in the worksheet.

✓ Move the pointer to the bottom of the window. As you reach the bottom, keep pressing the **<Down>** key. The pointer doesn't seem to move down, but notice that the row numbers on the left side change. The worksheet moves upward allowing your window view to move down over the worksheet.

✓ Move the pointer to the right and notice how the worksheet column letters change as you drag the worksheet behind the window.

✓ Press the **<Home>** key and immediately the window moves to the top left corner of the worksheet. Cell A1 is the home position.

✓ Press the **<F5>** function key. Notice the second line of the control panel requests a cell address. Type D10 (use the numbers at the top of the keyboard) and then press the **<Return>** key. Did the pointer jump directly to cell D10? This method allows you to move directly to any cell on the worksheet.

As you have noticed, only a small section of the total worksheet can be viewed through the window. Moving an entire page is a very easy task using the page-movement keys shown in the diagram.

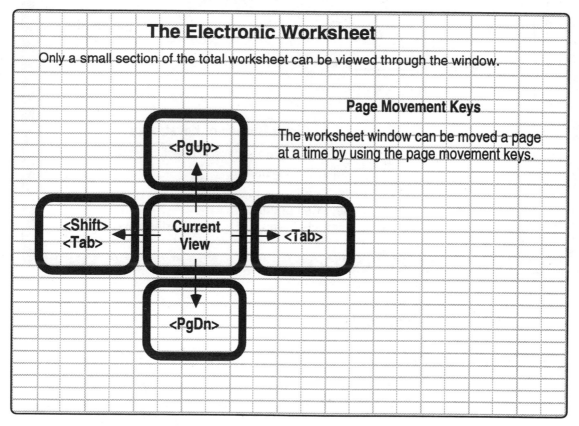

Practice page movements.

✓ Using the page movement keys, practice turning pages. 1-2-3 beeps when you hit the edge of the worksheet.

✓ When you have finished practicing the page movements, press the **<Home>** key to return to cell A1.

Typing Labels and Values

After moving to a particular cell, you will often enter data into the cell. When the mode indicator shows READY, data entry is accomplished by typing the data and then pressing the **<Return>** key to complete the entry. The data will be either a label or a value. Labels consist of descriptive titles that are not used in worksheet calculations. Values consist of numbers, formulas, or functions, all of which are used in worksheet calculations.

When the first character is typed, 1-2-3 decides whether you are entering a label or a value and indicates this in the mode indicator at the top right corner of the control panel. The mode indicator changes from READY to either LABEL or VALUE, depending on the first character you type. In general, a letter will indicate a label and a number or arithmetic operator such as a plus sign will indicate a value.

While typing labels or values, if you make a mistake *before* pressing the **<Return>** key, simply press the **<Backspace>** key to erase the mistake and then continue. To erase the entire line, press the **<Escape>** key and start over. If you notice the mistake *after* you have pressed the **<Return>** key, move to the cell, retype the data, and press the **<Return>** key. Later you will learn to edit a cell's contents without retyping the entire entry.

You must place 1-2-3 in the READY mode before you can enter labels or values. If the mode indicator (top right-hand corner) does not indicate READY, press the **<Escape>** key until it does. Usually once will do it, but occasionally you must press the **<Escape>** key more than once.

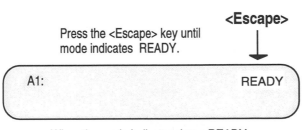

Press the <Escape> key until mode indicates READY.

<Escape>

| A1: | READY |

When the mode indicator shows READY
you can enter either labels or values.

Practice typing labels.

✓ Move to cell A2 and type your name. Notice that the mode indicator changes to LABEL and that the label is displayed on the second line of the control panel as you type it. Now press the **<Return>** key and your name will be entered in the worksheet in cell A2. Also, your name will be moved from the second line to the first line of the control panel and the mode will change from LABEL back to READY.

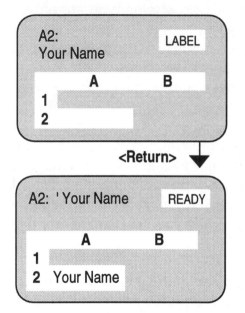

When in READY mode, your first keystroke will change the mode. If it is a letter, the mode will change to LABEL.

Pressing <Return> enters the label into cell A2 and moves the label from line 2 to line 1 of the control panel. Mode changes back to READY.

✓ Move to the appropriate cells and enter the rest of the labels shown below.

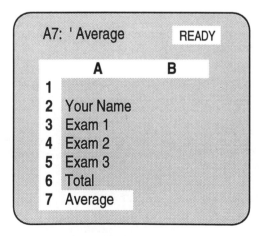

Practice typing numeric values.

✓ Use the numbers at the top of the keyboard for typing numbers. Move to cell B3 and type the number 89, representing the points earned on your first accounting exam. The mode indicator changes to VALUE when you type the number 8. 1-2-3 indicates VALUE to let you know that it thinks you are entering a value that can be used in calculations. Remember, values can be used in calculations, but labels cannot be. Press the **<Return>** key to enter this value into cell B3 and return to the READY mode.

✓ Move to the appropriate cells and enter the rest of the exam scores shown below.

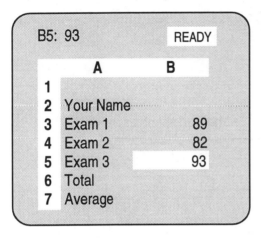

	A	B
	B5: 93	READY
1		
2	Your Name	
3	Exam 1	89
4	Exam 2	82
5	Exam 3	93
6	Total	
7	Average	

✓ At this point, you may be tempted to add the three exam scores and then type the total in cell B6. Don't! 1-2-3 can do math better than the best math student. Although 1-2-3 is very fast at math, it is not very smart at knowing how to relate the various cells. Using formulas, you will tell 1-2-3 which cells to add and which cells to average. This is where you have the upper hand. Unlike 1-2-3, you understand relationships and have the ability to control the flow of data. As you will see, combining your relationship skills and 1-2-3's math skills will be an unbeatable combination.

Practice typing formula values.

✓   Move to cell B6 and type the formula to add your three exam scores.
Type **+B3+B4+B5** and then press the **<Return>** key. The plus sign is typed first to alert
1-2-3 that your entry is a value. Your formula instructs 1-2-3 to add the values in cells B3,
B4, and B5. Because you started in cell B6, your formula will be stored in cell B6 and the
calculated result will be displayed in the worksheet at cell B6.

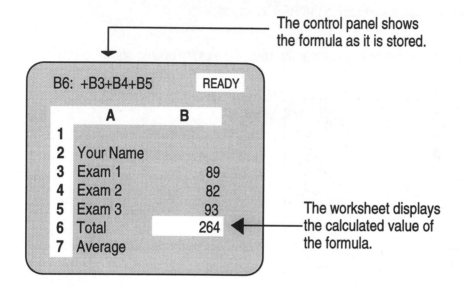

The control panel shows
the formula as it is stored.

The worksheet displays
the calculated value of
the formula.

✓   Move to cell B7 and type the formula to average your three exam scores.
Type **(B3+B4+B5)/3** and then press the **<Return>** key. The left parenthesis is typed first to
alert 1-2-3 that your entry is a value. Your formula instructs 1-2-3 to add the values in cells
B3, B4, and B5, and then to divide the total by 3. The slash before the three is used to
represent division. Because the cells B3, B4, and B5 are enclosed in parentheses, they will
be added first and then divided by 3. Because you started in cell B7, your formula will be
stored in cell B7 and the calculated result will be displayed in the worksheet at cell B7.

1-2-3 Math   The basic mathematical operators are:

Operators	Keys to use to avoid shifting
+ Add	The large key to the right of the **<PgDn>** key.
- Subtract	The key to the right of the **<PgUp>** key.
* Multiply	The asterisk key to the left of the **<End>** key.
/ Divide	The slash key to the left of the **<Shift>** key.

Practice typing functions.

✓   Functions are special formulas that are built into 1-2-3. Functions perform operations that would be either inconvenient or not possible to accomplish otherwise. For example, if you wanted to add or average a long list of numbers, typing each cell address would be very inconvenient.

✓   Move to cell B6 and type a function to add your three exam scores. (This function will replace your formula entered in the prior practice exercise.)
Type **@SUM(B3.B5)** and press the **<Return>** key. All functions begin with the **@** sign. This is a signal to 1-2-3 that you are entering a value in the form of a built-in function. The next three letters SUM tell 1-2-3 which function to use—in this case, the function to sum a list of numbers. The last part, enclosed in parentheses, includes the beginning cell and the ending cell separated by a period.

✓   Move to cell B7 and type a function to average your three exam scores. (This function will replace your formula entered in the prior practice exercise.)
Type **@AVG(B3.B5)** and press the **<Return>** key. All functions begin with the **@** sign. This signals 1-2-3 that you would like to average the list of cells enclosed in parentheses. Notice that when the function is moved from the second line to the first line of the control panel, 1-2-3 places another period between the cell list. Also, if you type lower case letters for the cell column, 1-2-3 will convert them to uppercase. Not using the **<Shift>** key will facilitate data entry. Shifting is tricky, especially on the left side.

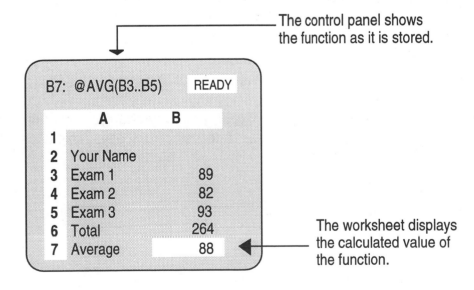

The control panel shows the function as it is stored.

	A	B
B7: @AVG(B3..B5)		READY
1		
2	Your Name	
3	Exam 1	89
4	Exam 2	82
5	Exam 3	93
6	Total	264
7	Average	88

The worksheet displays the calculated value of the function.

Practice changing numbers.

✓   Move to cell B3 and give yourself a score of 93. Did this change produce an average high enough for you? If not, change either of the other two inputs (cells B4 and B5) and notice the results. Be careful! It is tempting to type a number for the total or the average. This would defeat the purpose of the spreadsheet. Let the formulas or the functions do this work for you. The ability to change the input numbers and to see the results instantly is called "<u>what-if</u>" analysis or "<u>sensitivity</u>" analysis. For example, what if we change the Exam 1 score to 95, what will the average score be? Or how sensitive is the average to a change in one of the exam scores? This provides tremendous power for the problem solver, power that is not available with manual calculations.

Typing Summary

◆   **Labels** provide descriptive information only and are not used in calculations.

◆   **Values** may consist of numbers, formulas, or functions.

◆   **Numbers** represent the inputs to the problem.

◆   **Formulas** are computer instructions for calculating the outputs to the problem.

◆   **Functions** represent special formulas that are built into <u>1-2-3</u>. They provide a convenient way to accomplish otherwise difficult tasks.

◆   Once the spreadsheet program is complete, you may change any of the input numbers and the outputs will be updated electronically. This is called "<u>what-if</u>" or "<u>sensitivity</u>" analysis.

Selecting from the 1-2-3 Command Menu

In addition to moving around the worksheet and typing labels and values, you can perform many other tasks using 1-2-3's command menus. Selecting from the menu may sound like you will be dining out, and in a sense you will be. 1-2-3 offers hundreds of options to choose from. Understanding and using these menus presents a real challenge and provides a powerful tool for the serious electronic spreadsheet user.

The menus are organized like a tree structure. You always start at the trunk (the main menu), then work your way up the tree, choosing one branch (sub-menus) over another, then another, and another until you finally reach the top level with nowhere to go. This ends your selection process and completes the operation, returning to the trunk. Like a tree, the path from the bottom to the top will vary with each command: some paths are short, others are much longer.

Selecting from the main menu is easy. First you request the menu list and then you enter your selection. Based on your selection, 1-2-3 then provides additional submenus from which you will have an opportunity to select more options, and so on.

Requesting the Main Menu

You must place 1-2-3 in the READY mode before you can request the main menu. If the mode indicator (top right-hand corner) does not indicate READY, press the **<Escape>** key until it does. Usually once will do it, but occasionally you must press the **<Escape>** key more than once.

Now that 1-2-3 is READY, you press the **</>** slash key (lower right by the Shift key). This is your request for 1-2-3 to display the main menu. The main menu is instantly displayed in lines 2 and 3 of the control panel. The mode now indicates MENU, meaning that 1-2-3 is waiting for you to select one of the commands listed in line 2. The first command **Worksheet** is highlighted. The third line describes what the Worksheet command will accomplish.

When the main menu is displayed, you can press the **<Right>** arrow key to highlight the next option. You will notice that the third line will now display a description or a submenu of the highlighted option.

Practice requesting the Main Menu.

✓ First, place 1-2-3 in the READY mode. Then request the main menu by pressing the </> slash key, instantly placing 1-2-3 in the MENU mode and displaying the main menu on line 2 with a description of the Worksheet command on line 3. Press the **<Escape>** key to clear the second and third lines of the control panel, and return to the READY mode.

When the mode indicator shows READY . . .

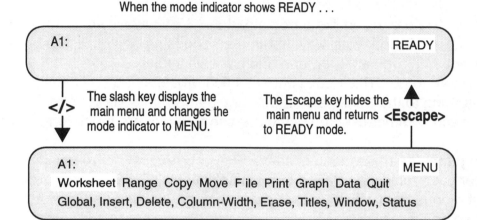

A1:   READY

The slash key displays the   The Escape key hides the
</> main menu and changes the   main menu and returns **<Escape>**
     mode indicator to MENU.   to READY mode.

A1:   MENU
Worksheet Range Copy Move F ile Print Graph Data Quit
Global, Insert, Delete, Column-Width, Erase, Titles, Window, Status

✓ Alternately press the </> key and the **<Escape>** key while keeping an eye on the mode indicator. A single keystroke communicates your request to either display or hide the main menu.

NOTE: Watch the worksheet window! As you request the main menu and select commands, try to look at the worksheet window, especially the control panel, as you press the keys. If you must study the keyboard to find the right key, please look up before pressing it. If you type the keystrokes while looking at the keyboard, you will miss all of the action and lose the learning potential provided by the window activity.

Selecting from the Main Menu

Requesting the main menu is easy. Knowing which item to select is more difficult. Of course, your selection will depend on what you want to accomplish. The following list briefly describes the main menu list.

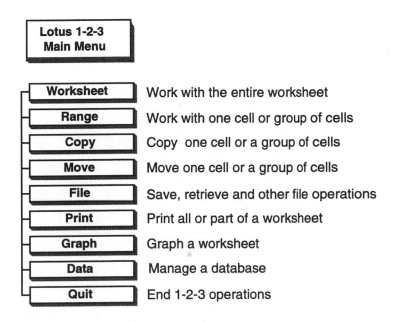

Lotus 1-2-3 Main Menu	
Worksheet	Work with the entire worksheet
Range	Work with one cell or group of cells
Copy	Copy one cell or a group of cells
Move	Move one cell or a group of cells
File	Save, retrieve and other file operations
Print	Print all or part of a worksheet
Graph	Graph a worksheet
Data	Manage a database
Quit	End 1-2-3 operations

You can select from the menus in one of two ways:

(1) The "point and pick" method. Point to your selection by pressing the **<Right>** arrow key and then pick the selection by pressing the **<Return>** key.

OR

(2) The "direct pick" method. Simply press the first letter of the command you want to select. No **<Return>** is necessary. You will find this method to be the quickest and the most direct.

The first method was designed for the beginner and the second for the experienced user.

Practice menu selections.

✓ Request the main menu. Using the **<Right>** arrow key, highlight the menu choices in line 2 of the control panel. As each choice is highlighted, read the third line of the control panel to get an idea of the type of operation each command performs. When the last command, **Quit,** is highlighted, press the **<Right>** key again. Does the menu pointer disappear, or did it return to the beginning? Highlight the first option **Worksheet** and then press the **<Left>** arrow key. Did the menu pointer jump to the end of the list? As you can see, the menu options are arranged in a circle, moving from the end to the beginning or from the beginning to the end, depending on which direction you point with the arrow keys.

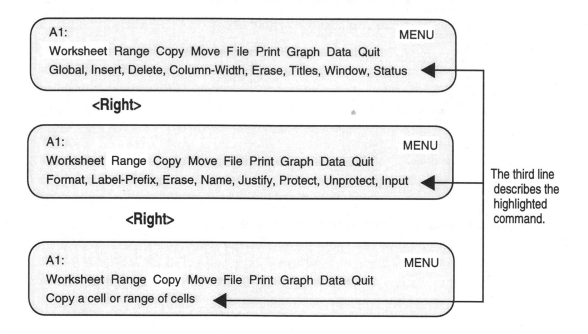

A1:   MENU
Worksheet Range Copy Move F ile Print Graph Data Quit
Global, Insert, Delete, Column-Width, Erase, Titles, Window, Status ◀

<Right>

A1:   MENU
Worksheet Range Copy Move File Print Graph Data Quit
Format, Label-Prefix, Erase, Name, Justify, Protect, Unprotect, Input ◀   The third line
                                                                               describes the
                                                                               highlighted
                                                                               command.
<Right>

A1:   MENU
Worksheet Range Copy Move File Print Graph Data Quit
Copy a cell or range of cells ◀

✓ Highlight the **Range** command. Press the **<Return>** key to display the submenu for the Range command. Notice that the submenus are now displayed on the second line of the control panel with a description of the highlighted command showing on the third line. Now use the **<Right>** arrow key to highlight the submenu commands while reading the description in the third line. This is the same procedure you used for the main menu commands. Now highlight the **Label-Prefix** command and then press the **<Return>** key. Another submenu appears with the options **Left**, **Right**, and **Center**. Using the **<Right>** arrow key, you can highlight any of these options while reading the description in the third line. Press the **<Escape>** key to return to the **Range** submenu. Press the **<Escape>** key again to return to the main menu and finally press the **<Escape>** key to return to the READY mode.

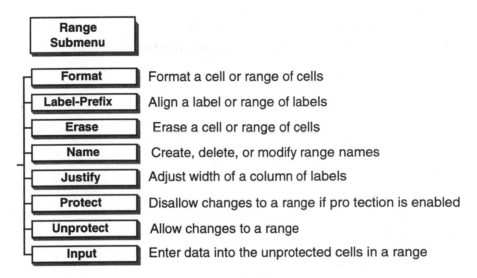

Range Submenu	
Format	Format a cell or range of cells
Label-Prefix	Align a label or range of labels
Erase	Erase a cell or range of cells
Name	Create, delete, or modify range names
Justify	Adjust width of a column of labels
Protect	Disallow changes to a range if pro tection is enabled
Unprotect	Allow changes to a range
Input	Enter data into the unprotected cells in a range

✓ Fortunately, there is an easier way to select menu and submenu commands: the "direct pick" method. Let's try it. Start in the READY mode. Press the **</>** slash key, and then select the **Range** command by pressing the letter **R**. Now select the **Label-Prefix** command by pressing the letter **L**. You should be looking at the options **Left, Right, and Center**. The shorthand for this will be as follows:

Select: **/ R L** .... Range Label-Prefix command.

You will use this method in the sample problems that follow.

IMPORTANT: Remember that if you make a mistake, you can back up one level by pressing the **<Escape>** key. Also, you can go directly to the READY mode without using a series of escape keystrokes. While holding down the **<Ctrl>** key with the left hand, press the **<ScrollLock>** key with the right hand and release both keys. Presto! You are back to READY. Try it!

Practice saving your work to the disk.

✓ You can save your work at any time by selecting the **File** command from the main menu. Are your exam scores still displayed in the worksheet window? If not, enter your name and any other data you wish into a blank worksheet. Then do the following:

Select: **/ F S** .... File Save command
Type: **GRADES** .... Your file name must be eight letters or less, either upper or lowercase. <u>1-2-3</u> will convert to uppercase.
Press: **<Return>** .... To complete save command, and return to READY.

The disk drive light will glow and your work will be written to your floppy disk. Your work is still displayed in the window. Saving your work means saving an exact copy of your displayed worksheet onto the floppy disk.

Practice retrieving your work from the disk.

✓ Make a few changes to your displayed worksheet. If your worksheet shows your exam scores, give yourself three perfect scores. Now do the following:

Select: **/ F R** .... File Retrieve command
Type: **GRADES** .... Your file name. (If 1-2-3 cannot find the file you will hear a beep with a message at the bottom. Press **<Return>** to continue.)
Press: **<Return>** .... To complete retrieve command, and return to READY.

The disk drive light will glow and your previously saved work will be displayed. Are your three perfect exam scores shown? You will see that all of your work since your last save has been lost. Because 1-2-3 can only display one worksheet at a time, the current worksheet will be replaced by the retrieved file.

WARNING: Do not retrieve a worksheet without first saving your current work, or you may lose much more than three perfect scores.

Practice ending a 1-2-3 session.

✓   Make sure you have saved your work and are in the READY mode. Then

Select: **/ Q** .... **Q**uit command.
Select: **Y** .... **Y**es option to confirm.

You will return to the **Lotus Access System.** Then

Select: **E**................. **E**xit command.
Select: **Y** .... **Y**es option to confirm.
You will return to the operating system, displaying **A>**.

✓   Remove your disks and return them to their protective jackets, or
restart Lotus by typing **Lotus** and then pressing the **<Return>** key.

Selecting Summary

◆   You can perform many tasks by selecting commands from 1-2-3's command
menus.

◆   The command menus are organized like a tree structure. You move from
the main menu to submenus, which can be three to five levels deep,
depending on the path you choose.

◆   You have two methods to select commands. Highlight your choice, and
then press the **<Return>** key, *or* press the first letter of the command which
moves you directly to the next submenu level.

◆   For the best learning situation, keep your eye on the worksheet window
while pressing the select keys.

◆   Remember to save your work before retrieving a file or ending 1-2-3.

Solving Business Problems Electronically

There are four steps to understanding and using electronic spreadsheets. The steps outlined below will be used in the sample problems that follow. You can complete steps 1 and 2 without using the computer. You will use the computer to complete steps 3 and 4.

1 **Solve** **the problem manually.**

Most business problems can be divided into two parts: data that are given (the inputs) and data that will be calculated (the outputs). The bridge between the known and the unknown depends on how well you understand the problem and your ability to establish relationships between the data elements. Solving the problem manually will help you determine these relationships.

2 **Program** **the relationships.**

After solving the problem manually, you will be ready to explicitly declare the relationships between the problem inputs and the problem outputs. These relationships are expressed with formulas.

3 **Create** **the electronic spreadsheet.**

Now that you have solved and programmed the problem, you are ready to use the computer. Using your spreadsheet skills such as moving, typing, and selecting, you will establish an electronic version of your manual worksheet.

4 **Analyze** **your solutions.**

Verify your electronic program by comparing your electronic output with your manual calculations. Once you are satisfied that your program is correct, you are ready to use the worksheet for its intended purpose: processing data electronically. Changing the inputs will instantly produce the related outputs, allowing you to experiment with an almost endless variety of situations. This process will further enhance your understanding of the problem.

Simple Income Statement

Solve the problem manually.

This problem consists of two inputs and two related outputs. The numeric inputs to the problem are given and the required calculations are enclosed by boxes. Using a pencil and calculator, compute the manual worksheet. Write your answers directly in the boxed areas for cells B6 and B8.

	A	B	C
1	Preparer's Name:		
2	Spreadsheet Title:	Income Statement	
3		JAN	
4	Revenue	120,000	
5	Expense	78,000	
6	Net Income		
7			
8	Profit Percentage		

Independent Inputs

B4 Revenue
B5 Expense

Dependent Outputs

B6 Net Income
B8 Profit Percentage

Program the relationships.

You will now establish the relationships that you used to calculate your answers. Relationships are expressed as formulas. Enter your formulas for cells B6 and B8 in the boxes below.

Cell Description	Cell	Formula
Net Income	B6	
Profit Percentage	B8	

Net income is determined by subtracting expense (cell B5) from revenue (cell B4). This would be written as **+B4-B5** (the plus sign is added in front to alert the computer that a value is being entered rather than a label). Did you have trouble expressing the formula for profit percentage? You will soon find out that only relationships that are understood manually can be programmed electronically. The value for profit percentage is determined by dividing net income (cell B6) by revenue (cell B4). This is written as **+B6/B4** (the Slash key is used to represent division).

Create the Simple Income Statement.

1 **BEGIN WITH A BLANK WORKSHEET.**

Load *Lotus 1-2-3* if not already loaded,
   or
if <u>1-2-3</u> is already displayed, then
Select: **/ W E Y** .... Worksheet Erase Yes command.
   Reminder: If needed, save your work before erasing.

2 **ENTER LABELS IN COLUMN A.**

Using the arrow keys, move to the appropriate cell and type the label;
   then
Press: **<Down>** or **<Return>** .... To complete the entry.
Pressing the **<Down>** key will enter the label into the cell <u>and</u> move down to the next cell.
Pressing the **<Return>** key will enter the label into the cell but stays in the same location.

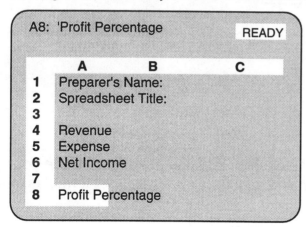

Because a column's width is originally set for nine characters, some of the labels in column A do not fit. These labels spill over into column B. Since the cells in column B are empty, they have soft cell boundaries allowing the contents of column A cells to be displayed. In step 3, you will widen column A.

Erasing a cell's contents.

If you, make a mistake, you can erase the contents of any cell, or group of cells, by moving to the cell and then

Select: **/ R E**..............................Range Erase command
Press: **<Return>**........................To erase a single cell or point to a range and then press
                                          the **<Return>** key for a group of cells.

WIDEN COLUMN A.

Move: **A8**...................... The pointer can be in any row in column A.
Select: **/ W C**................... **W**orksheet **C**olumn-Width command.
Select: **S**........................ **S**et option

The control panel (shown below) shows the current width to be 9 characters with a possible width of from 1-72 characters. The mode indicates POINT which means that you can use the **<Left>** or **<Right>** arrow keys to point the direction of either contraction or expansion.

> A8: 'Profit Percentage   POINT
> Enter column width (1..72): 9

Press: **<Right>**................ To expand column width one character. Continue pressing until the label is covered plus one or two extra spaces.
Press: **<Return>**.............. To complete the command, return to READY mode.

 ENTER LABELS IN COLUMN B.

Using the arrow keys, move to the appropriate cell and type the label;
then
Press: **<Down>** or **<Return>** .... To complete the entry.

Be sure to enter your name and other identifying information in cell B1.

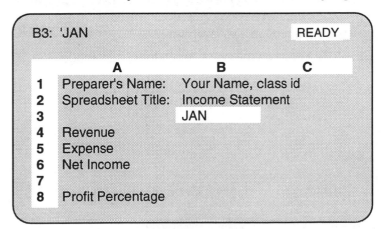

> B3: 'JAN   READY
>
> | | A | B | C |
> |---|---|---|---|
> | 1 | Preparer's Name: | Your Name, class id | |
> | 2 | Spreadsheet Title: | Income Statement | |
> | 3 | | JAN | |
> | 4 | Revenue | | |
> | 5 | Expense | | |
> | 6 | Net Income | | |
> | 7 | | | |
> | 8 | Profit Percentage | | |

Have you noticed that all labels are automatically aligned to the left of the cell? Notice that the cell contents shown in the first line of the control panel includes an apostrophe before the label but not in the worksheet. The apostrophe is the default alignment character. In step 8 you will center the contents of cell B3.

ENTER THE NUMERIC INPUTS.

Move:	**B4**......................	JAN Revenue
Type:	**120000**	Do not enter a comma; use numbers at top of keyboard.
Press:	**<Down>**..............	Enters number in cell B4 <u>and</u> moves to cell B5.
Type:	**78000**...................	Do not enter a comma; use numbers at top of keyboard.
Press:	**<Return>**............	To complete the entry, return to READY mode.

```
B5: 78000                                    READY

           A                 B           C
  1   Preparer's Name:   Your Name, class id
  2   Spreadsheet Title: Income Statement
  3                      JAN
  4   Revenue                  120000
  5   Expense                   78000
  6   Net Income
  7
  8   Profit Percentage
```

 ENTER THE FORMULAS.

Move:	**B6**......................	JAN Net Income
Type:	**+B4-B5**	Use the plus key to begin a formula, the Minus key to subtract.
Press:	**<Down>** 2 times......	Enters formula in cell B6 <u>and</u> moves to cell B8. Press the **<Down>** key twice.
Type:	**+B6/B4**	Use the Slash key for division.
Press:	**<Return>**	To complete the entry, return to READY mode.

```
B8: +B6/B4                                   READY

           A                 B           C
  1   Preparer's Name:   Your Name, class id
  2   Spreadsheet Title: Income Statement
  3                      JAN
  4   Revenue                  120000
  5   Expense                   78000
  6   Net Income                42000
  7
  8   Profit Percentage         0.35
```

FORMAT THE NUMBERS DISPLAYED IN THE WORKSHEET.

Format Dollars

Move:	**B4**......................	First dollar amount.
Select:	**/ R F**....................	**R**ange **F**ormat command.
Select:	**,**........................	**C**omma option.
Type:	**0**......................	Zero decimals.
Press:	**\<Return\>**.............	Enters decimal option.
Press:	**\<Down\>** 2 times.....	To expand range to include cell B6.
Press:	**\<Return\>**.............	To complete command, return to READY mode.

The format is shown in parentheses before the number 120000. The format is commas with zero decimals.

```
B4:  (,0)  120000                           READY

              A              B            C
  1   Preparer's Name:   Your Name, class id
  2   Spreadsheet Title: Income Statement
  3                      JAN
  4   Revenue                120,000
  5   Expense                 78,000
  6   Net Income              42,000
  7
  8   Profit Percentage         0.35
```

Format Percent

Move:	**B8**......................	Profit percentage.
Select:	**/ R F**....................	**R**ange **F**ormat command.
Select:	**P**........................	**P**ercent option.
Press:	**\<Return\>**.............	Accepts suggested 2 decimal places.
Press:	**\<Return\>**.............	Completes command, returns to READY mode.

The format is shown in parentheses before the formula for cell B8. The format is percent with two decimals. (P2)

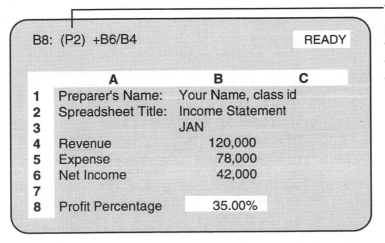

```
B8:  (P2)  +B6/B4                           READY

              A              B            C
  1   Preparer's Name:   Your Name, class id
  2   Spreadsheet Title: Income Statement
  3                      JAN
  4   Revenue                120,000
  5   Expense                 78,000
  6   Net Income              42,000
  7
  8   Profit Percentage        35.00%
```

8 ALIGN LABELS.

Press:	**\<Home\>**	Pointer goes to cell A1, the home base.
Select:	**/ R L**	**R**ange **L**abel command.
Select:	**R**	**R**ight alignment option.
Press:	**\<Down\>**	Expands range to include cell A2.
Press:	**\<Return\>**	To complete command, return to READY mode.
Move:	**B3**	JAN label
Select:	**/ R L**	**R**ange **L**abel command.
Select:	**C**	**C**enter alignment option.
Press:	**\<Return\>**	To complete command, return to READY mode.

Notice the caret (small cap) before the label. This symbol is for center alignment .

B3: ^JAN   READY

	A	B	C
1	Preparer's Name:	Your Name, class id	
2	Spreadsheet Title:	Income Statement	
3		JAN	
4	Revenue	120,000	
5	Expense	78,000	
6	Net Income	42,000	
7			
8	Profit Percentage	35.00%	

Aligning Labels

Labels can be aligned when they are entered by typing one of the alignment symbols as the first character.

'	Apostrophe	**Left alignment** (if no character is entered this will be used)
^	Caret (Shift 6)	**Center alignment**
"	Double quote	**Right alignment**

9 SAVE YOUR WORK.

Press:	**\<Home\>**	Pointer goes to cell A1, the home base.
Select:	**/ F S**	**F**ile **S**ave command.
Type:	**SIS**	File name can be up to 8 characters long. Special characters or spaces are not allowed.
Press:	**\<Return\>**	To complete command, return to READY mode.

Name:_____ Class:_____ Date:_____

File: **SIS**   Title: **Simple Income Statement**

[Analyze] **your solutions.**

VERIFY YOUR WORK. Compare your electronic and manual solutions.

(1) What is the net income for January? $_____

(2) What is the profit percentage for January? _____%

PREDICT RESULTS. Without using the computer, answer these questions.

(3) If January expense is increased by $10,000, net income would be $_____ and the profit percentage would _____(increase/decrease).

PERFORM "WHAT-IF" ANALYSIS. Using the computer, confirm your predictions and then answer the questions below.

(4) If January revenue is $289,000 and expense is $196,300, then net income is $_____ and profit percentage is _____%.

(5) If January revenue is $489,280 and expense is $329,530, then net income is $_____ and profit percentage is _____%.

Quarterly Income Statement

Solve the problem manually.

This problem is an expansion of the previous sample problem, the Simple Income Statement, which had two inputs and two calculated outputs. This problem is expanded for 6 inputs and 10 outputs. Using a pencil and calculator, complete the worksheet by writing your answers directly in the boxes that represent the 10 outputs.

	A	B	C	D	E
1	Preparer's Name:				
2	Spreadsheet Title:	Quarterly Income Statement			
3		JAN	FEB	MAR	TOTAL
4	Revenue	120,000	135,000	160,000	
5	Expense	78,000	91,800	118,400	
6	Net Income				
7					
8	Profit Percentage				

Program the relationships.

Complete the table below, writing the formulas for the 10 output calculations.

Cell Description	Cell	Formula
Total Revenue	E4	@SUM( )
Total Expense	E5	@SUM( )
JAN Net Income	B6	
FEB Net Income	C6	
MAR Net Income	D6	
Total Net Income	E6	
JAN Profit Percentage	B8	
FEB Profit Percentage	C8	
MAR Profit Percentage	D8	
Total Profit Percentage	E8	

Before you enter these formulas into your worksheet, let's discuss a few of your options. You'll be able to return to the keyboard in a moment.

Like any programming activity, programming a spreadsheet is an art. This implies that different techniques and styles can be used. Let's consider two approaches.

First approach - Type the 10 formulas.

The 10 formulas could be typed in the appropriate worksheet cells. If you are a great typist, this method may appeal to you. However, you will find that typing the cell address is not only tedious but also subject to error.

Second approach - Type the primary formulas, copy the relative formulas.

You will notice a similarity in some of your formulas as follows:

Total formulas - The column letters are the same; the row numbers are different.

Cell Description	Cell	Formula	
Total Revenue	E4	@SUM(B4 .. D4)	Relative formula: Add the three cells to the left.
Total Expense	E5	@SUM(B5 .. D5)	

Net income formulas - The rows are the same; the columns are different.

Cell Description	Cell	Formula	
JAN Net Income	B6	+ B4 - B5	
FEB Net Income	C6	+ C4 - C5	Relative formula: Subtract the cell above from the cell two rows above.
MAR Net Income	D6	+ D4 - D5	
Total Net Income	E6	+ E4 - E5	

Profit percentage formulas - The rows are the same; the columns are different.

Cell Description	Cell	Formula	
JAN Profit Percentage	B8	+ B6 / B4	
FEB Profit Percentage	C8	+ C6 / C4	Relative formula: Divide the cell two rows above by the cell four rows above.
MAR Profit Percentage	D8	+ D6 / D4	
Total Profit Percentage	E8	+ E6 / E4	

A **primary** formula is a formula that represents of a group of related or similar formulas. In the table above, the first formula in each of the three groups could be treated as primary. This means that it would be entered first, either by typing or pointing to the cell addresses. The related formulas would then be entered by copying the primary formula. The following table illustrates this approach.

Cell Description	Cell	Primary Formula	Copy To
Total Revenue	E4	@SUM(B4 .. D4)	E5
JAN Net Income	B6	+ B4 - B5	C6..E6
JAN Profit Percentage	B8	+ B6 / B4	C8..E8

Create the Quarterly Income Statement.

1 **BEGIN WITH THE SIMPLE INCOME STATEMENT.**
Load <u>Lotus 1-2-3</u> if not already loaded,
> **or**

if <u>1-2-3</u> is already displayed,
> **then**

Select: **/ F R** .... File **R**etreive command.
Type: **SIS** .... File saved in prior example.
Press: **<Return>** .... To complete command.

A1: "Preparer's Name:		READY
	A	**B**	**C**
1	Preparer's Name:	Your Name, class id	
2	Spreadsheet Title:	Income Statement	
3		JAN	
4	Revenue	120,000	
5	Expense	78,000	
6	Net Income	42,000	
7			
8	Profit Percentage	35.00%	

EDIT THE SPREADSHEET TITLE.
Move: **B2**........................ The cell to edit.
Press: **<F2>**.................... To begin the EDIT mode. Look at the second line of the control panel. This is where you will edit the title.
Press: **<Left>** 16 times ..... Continue pressing until the small edit pointer is at the point where you would like to add characters (under the I). The apostrophe is the left alignment symbol. Leave this at the beginning.
Type: **Quarterly** .... To insert additional characters at the pointer (include the space after "Quarterly").
Press: **<Return>** .... To complete the edit and return to READY or press **<Escape>** to ignore and try again.

NOTE: You can use the function key **<F2>** to edit the contents of any cell, label, or value. Press the **<Del>** delete key to erase the character over the edit pointer (second line of the control panel), and then type a character to insert at the edit pointer. Press the **<Return>** key to replace the old cell contents with the new contents or press the **<Escape>** key to ignore your changes.

COPY THE JANUARY INCOME STATEMENT.

Move: **B3** .... The first cell to copy.
Select: **/ C** .... Copy command.
Press: **<Down>** 5 times..... To expand FROM range to include cells B3 thru B8

B8: (P2) +B6/B4   POINT
Enter range to copy FROM: B3..B8

	A	B	C	D	E
1	Preparer's Name:	Your Name, class id			
2	Spreadsheet Title:	Quarterly Income Statement			
3		JAN			
4	Revenue	120,000			
5	Expense	78,000			
6	Net Income	42,000			
7					
8	Profit Percentage	35.00%			

Press: **<Return>** .... To complete FROM range.
Press: **<Right>** .... To begin TO range at cell C3.
Type: .... Type a period to anchor the begin TO range at cell C3.
Press: **<Right>** 2 times...... To include cells C3 thru E3.
Press: **<Return>** .... To complete the Copy command.

B3: ^JAN   READY

	A	B	C	D	E
1	Preparer's Name:	Your Name, class id			
2	Spreadsheet Title:	Quarterly Income Statement			
3		JAN	JAN	JAN	JAN
4	Revenue	120,000	120,000	120,000	120,000
5	Expense	78,000	78,000	78,000	78,000
6	Net Income	42,000	42,000	42,000	42,000
7					
8	Profit Percentage	35.00%	35.00%	35.00%	35.00%

NOTE: Your worksheet now includes the proper formulas for net income and profit percentage for the quarter. As a bonus, the format for dollars and percent have been carried over to the appropriate cells. Next you will change the labels for the months and the numeric inputs.

3 CORRECT THE COLUMN LABELS.

Using the center alignment symbol, type the correct labels.

Move:	**C3**	
Type:	**^FEB**	The caret (shift number 6) will center the label.
Press:	**<Right>**	To move to cell D3.
Type:	**^MAR**	Correct label
Press:	**<Right>**	To move to cell D3.
Type:	**^TOTAL**	Correct label.
Press:	**<Return>**	To enter label.

4 CORRECT THE NUMBERS FOR FEBRUARY AND MARCH.

Using the arrow keys enter the correct numbers for revenue and expense for FEB and MAR. Remember, use the numbers at the top of the keyboard and do not enter a comma. Do **not** enter the numbers for net income and profit percentage. As you enter the correct numbers for revenue and expense, the net income and profit percentage will be electronically updated based on the formulas that were copied from step 2.

D5: (,0) 118400   READY

	A	B	C	D	E
1	Preparer's Name: Your Name, class id				
2	Spreadsheet Title: Quarterly Income Statement				
3		JAN	FEB	MAR	TOTAL
4	Revenue	120,000	135,000	160,000	120,000
5	Expense	78,000	91,800	118,400	78,000
6	Net Income	42,000	43,200	41,600	42,000
7					
8	Profit Percentage	35.00%	32.00%	26.00%	35.00%

These numbers are updated automatically.

Your numbers will be automatically formatted the same as the January numbers. The format was copied along with everything else. This is an added incentive to copy the relative formulas.

5 ENTER THE FORMULA FOR TOTAL REVENUE.

Formulas can be entered by either typing the cell references or by pointing to the cell references using the pointer movement keys. These two options are listed below. Compare the two options and then use **Option 2** (point to the cell references) to enter your formula for the total revenue.

Option 1 - Type the cell references.

Move:	**E4**	Total revenue.
Type:	**+B4+C4+D4**	Formula for total revenue.
Press:	**<Return>**	To complete command.

Option 2 - Point to the cell references.

Move:	**E4**	Total revenue.
Type:	**+**........................	Plus sign to begin the formula.
Press:	**<Left>** 3 times	To point to the first cell reference, cell B4.
Type:	**+**........................	To enter the next operator. Pointer jumps back to cell E4.
Press:	**<Left>** 2 times......	To point to the next cell reference, cell C4.
Type:	**+**........................	To enter the next operator. Pointer jumps back to cell E4.
Press:	**<Left>**	To point to the last cell reference, cell D4.
Press:	**<Return>**	To complete the formula.

E4: (,0) +B4+C4+D4   READY

	A	B	C	D	E
1	Preparer's Name: Your Name, class id				
2	Spreadsheet Title: Quarterly Income Statement				
3		JAN	FEB	MAR	TOTAL
4	Revenue	120,000	135,000	160,000	415,000
5	Expense	78,000	91,800	118,400	78,000
6	Net Income	42,000	43,200	41,600	337,000
7					
8	Profit Percentage	35.00%	32.00%	26.00%	81.20%

6 ENTER THE FORMULA FOR TOTAL EXPENSE.

The formula for total expense can be entered using either of the two options outlined in step 5. However, it will be easier to copy the total revenue formula found in cell E4. Both cells E4 and E5 require the same relative formula, which is to add the three numbers to the left of the cell. Enter the formula using the copy method as shown:

Move: **E4** .... Total revenue.
Select: **/ C** .... **C**opy command.
Press: **<Return>** .... To complete FROM range.
Press: **<Down>**............... To begin TO range at cell E5.
Press: **<Return>** .... To complete the Copy command.

E4: (,0) +B4+C4+D4   READY

	A	B	C	D	E
1	Preparer's Name: Your Name, class id				
2	Spreadsheet Title: Quarterly Income Statement				
3		JAN	FEB	MAR	TOTAL
4	Revenue	120,000	135,000	160,000	415,000
5	Expense	78,000	91,800	118,400	288,200
6	Net Income	42,000	43,200	41,600	126,800
7					
8	Profit Percentage	35.00%	32.00%	26.00%	30.55%

DRESS UP YOUR WORKSHEET.

We can do a number of things to make the worksheet more presentable. Let's add double and single underlines and dollar signs.

Add double underlines between the column labels and the first numbers.

First, Insert a blank row

Move:	**B4**	Row 4. column B is where we will begin the underlines.
Select:	**/ W I R**...................	Worksheet Insert Row command.
Press:	**<Return>**	To enter a blank row, moving all rows down.

Next, fill cell B4 with double underlines.

Type:	**\ =**	Be careful, this is the backslash "repeat" key (left side of keyboard by the shift key) and an equal sign (double underline).
Press:	**<Return>**	To enter double underline across width of cell B4.

Finally, copy the underlines across to cell E4.

Select:	**/ C**	Copy command.
Press:	**<Return>**	To end FROM range.
Press:	**<Right>**	To begin TO range at cell C4.
Type:	**.**	Type a period to anchor cell C4 as the first cell in the TO range.
Press:	**<Right>** 2 times......	To expand range to include cell E4.
Press:	**<Return>**	To complete command.

Now repeat this procedure for a single underline beginning at cell B7. Insert a blank row above B7, enter a single underline (use the minus sign instead of the equal sign), and finally copy this across to column E.

Next, place a double underline at cell B9 across to cell E9. You do not need to insert a blank row; use the one already there.

Add dollar signs in row 5 and row 8.

Move:	**B5**......................	First dollar amount.
Select:	**/ R F**	Range Format command.
Select:	**C**.......................	Currency option.
Type:	**0**	Zero decimals.
Press:	**<Return>**	Enters decimal option.
Press:	**<Right>** 3 times.......	Expand range to include cell E5.
Press:	**<Return>**	Completes command, returns to READY mode.

Now do the same for row 8 and begin with cell B8.

```
B8: (C0) +B5-B6                                                    READY

              A           B          C          D          E
 1      Preparer's Name: Your Name, class id
 2      Spreadsheet Title: Quarterly Income Statement
 3                        JAN        FEB        MAR        TOTAL
 4                   ======================================================
 5   Revenue          $120,000   $135,000   $160,000   $415,000
 6   Expense            78,000     91,800    118,400    288,200
 7                   ------------------------------------------------------
 8   Net Income        $42,000    $43,200    $41,600   $126,800
 9                   ======================================================
10   Profit Percentage  35.00%     32.00%     26.00%     30.55%
```

 SAVE YOUR WORK.

Move: Position the pointer where you would like it to show when the file is retrieved later.

Select: **/ F S** .... File **S**ave command.

1-2-3 remembers that you started with a file named **SIS** and displays the file name on line two of the control panel. You could accept this name by pressing the **<Return>** key and selecting the option **R**eplace but this would erase the old file **SIS** and replace it with your updated worksheet. You can create a new file by simply typing a new file name. This leaves the old file **SIS** intact on the floppy disk.

Type: **QIS** .... File name.

Press: **<Return>** ..... Completes save command by writing the file to the disk. If there is already a file with the same name, you have an option to **R**eplace with the new version or **C**ancel the command.

PRINT YOUR COMPLETED SPREADSHEET.

You have many print options. Let's consider just three.

Option 1 - Print exactly what is shown on the screen, including the borders.
Move: Position the pointer wherever you would like.
Press: **<Shift><PrtSc>**..........While shifting, press the Print Screen key (right side).

Option 2 - Print a list of the cell contents as they are stored.
Move: Position the pointer where you would like it to show in the control panel.
Select: **/ P P**...............   **P**rint **P**rinter command.
Select: **O O C Q**.............   **O**ptions, **O**ther, **C**ell-Formulas, **Q**uit options.
Select: **R**.....................   **R**ange option.

> Point to the range desired, or select the entire spreadsheet by
> Press : **<Home>**............   Go to the cell A1.
> Type: **.**   ....   Period to anchor top cell.
> Press: **<End> <Home>**...   Go to the bottom. Press **<End>** and then **<Home>**.
> Press:**<Return>**...............   To enter the range.

Select: **A G**   ....   **A**lign **G**o options.
Select: **Q**   ....   **Q**uit option, return to READY mode.

Option 3 - Print a formal report.
Select: **/ P P** ....   **P**rint **P**rinter command.
Select: **O O A Q** ....   **O**ptions, **O**ther, **A**s-Displayed, **Q**uit options.
Select: **R** ....   **R**ange option.
Point to the range desired, or select the entire spreadsheet. See option 2 above.

Select: **A G** ....   **A**lign **G**o options

Preparer's Name: Your Name, class id
Spreadsheet Title: Quarterly Income Statement

	JAN	FEB	MAR	TOTAL
Revenue	$120,000	$135,000	$160,000	$415,000
Expense	78,000	91,800	118,400	288,200
Net Income	$42,000	$43,200	$41,600	$126,800
Profit Percentage	35.00%	32.00%	26.00%	30.55%

10 PROTECT YOUR COMPLETED SPREADSHEET.

Initially, all worksheet cells have protection status. This means that the cells are capable of being protected but that the protection switch has not been turned on. Once the protection is turned on, none of the cells can be changed. So the first step is to unprotect those cells that you wish to be able to change. When you analyze your solutions you will change the inputs to the problem; revenue and expense for January through March (cells B5 to D6). You can unprotect these input cell as follows:

Move: **B5**...................... January revenue.
Select: **/ R U** .... **R**ange **U**nprotect command.
Press: **<Down>**.............. Include B6.
Press: **<Right>** 2 times .... Expand range to include all input cells as shown.

```
D6: (,0) 118400                                          POINT
Enter range to unprotect: B5 . . D6

              A             B         C         D          E
 1    Preparer's Name: Your Name, class id
 2    Spreadsheet Title: Quarterly Income Statement
 3                         JAN       FEB       MAR       TOTAL
 4                      ===================================
 5    Revenue          $120,000  $135,000  $160,000   $415,000
 6    Expense            78,000    91,800   118,400    288,200
 7                      -----------------------------------
 8    Net Income        $42,000   $43,200   $41,600   $126,800
 9                      ===================================
10    Profit Percentage  35.00%    32.00%    26.00%    30.55%
```

Press: **<Return>**.............. To complete command.

The next step is to turn on the protection switch that will protect all cells that have not been explicitly unprotected. Do this as follows:

Select: **/ W G P** .... **W**orksheet **G**lobal **P**rotect command.
Select: **E**........................ **E**nable option.

Later, if you wish to turn the protection off, select the **D**isable option. After the protection has been turned on, some monitors will show the unprotected cells brighter (higher intensity) than the protected cells. You may need to adjust your monitor by turning the contrast knobs to get this effect. Now try to change any of the labels or values that have not been unprotected and you will find 1-2-3 unwilling to accept any modifications. Your spreadsheet is ready to be used without fear of inadvertently changing a label or a formula.

SAVE YOUR WORK AGAIN.

Move: Position the pointer where you would like it to show when the file is retrieved later.

Select: **/ F S** .... File Save command.

> Because your worksheet already has a name and has been previously saved to the disk, the current name is displayed after the prompt on the second line of the control panel. You can press the **<Return>** key to accept the name shown or you can type a new name. Let's use the old name.

Press: **<Return>** ..... To accept the old name.

> As a safety feature, you now have a choice. You can select the **R**eplace option or the **C**ancel option. Selecting **R**eplace will erase the old file and replace it with your new version. Selecting **C**ancel will ignore the Save command and return to the READY mode. If you are satisfied with your worksheet, select the **R**eplace option.

Select: **R** .... Replace option.

Remember to save your work after making significant changes. If you intend to use the same file name, use this sequence:

> Select: **/ F S**
> Press: **<Return>**
> Select: **R**

(12) GRAPH YOUR WORKSHEET.

The graphing capabilities of 1-2-3 are very impressive. Unfortunately, your computer may not be equipped to display graphics. Graphs can be printed but a separate disk is needed to accomplish this. You can execute the following instructions to see if your computer can display graphics.

First, indicate the type of graph you want to create.

Select:	**/ G T**	**G**raph **T**ype command.
Select:	**B**	**B**ar graph option.

Next, identify worksheet ranges to be graphed.

Select:	**X**	**X**-axis range command.
Move:	**B3**	JAN.
Type:	**.**	Type a period to anchor cell B3.
Press:	**<Right>** twice ...	To expand range to include D3.
Press:	**<Return>**	To complete command.

Select:	**A**	**A** option (first range of data).
Move:	**B5**	JAN Revenue.
Type:	**.**	Type a period to anchor cell B5.
Press:	**<Right>** twice ...	To expand range to include D5.
Press:	**<Return>**	To complete command.

Select:	**B**	**B** option (second range of data).
Move:	**B6**	JAN Expense.
Type:	**.**	Type a period to anchor cell B6.
Press:	**<Right>** twice ...	To expand range to include D6.
Press:	**<Return>**	To complete command.

Select:	**C**	**C** option (third range of data).
Move:	**B8**	JAN Net Income.
Type:	**.**	Type a period to anchor cell B8.
Press:	**<Right>** twice ...	To expand range to include D8.
Press:	**<Return>**	To complete command.
Select:	**Q**	**Q**uit option, return to READY mode.

Save your graph settings with the worksheet.

Select:	**/ F S**	**F**ile **S**ave command.
Press:	**<Return>**	To accept the old name.
Select:	**R**	**R**eplace option.

To look at the graph you've created:

Select: **/ G V** ....   **G**raph **V**iew command.

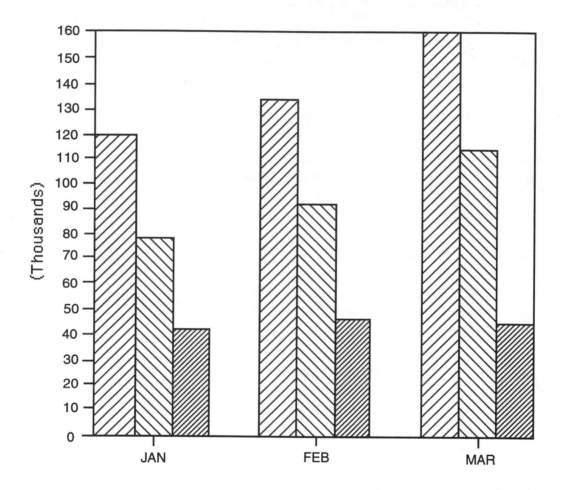

If your graph is not displayed, either your computer is not equipped with a graphics card or the Lotus 1-2-3 disk has not been installed to work with graphics. Because your graph settings have been saved, you may want to try viewing the graph with another computer.

Press: Any key ....   To return to graph commands.
Select: **Q** ....   **Q**uit option, return to READY mode.

(13) **LABEL AND DRESS UP THE GRAPH.**

If you have determined that your computer will display graphs, you may want to show labels and titles for readability. Try the following instructions.

Select: **/ G O** .... Graph Options command.

Set up legends.

Select: **L A** .... Legend option for **A** data range.
Type: **REVENUE**.......... To identify first bar for each month.
Press: **<Return>**.......... To enter the legend.

Select: **L B** .... Legend option for **B** data range.
Type: **EXPENSE**.......... To identify second bar for each month.
Press: **<Return>**.......... To enter the legend.

Select: **L C** .... Legend option for **C** data range.
Type: **NET INCOME** ..... To identify third bar for each month.
Press: **<Return>**.......... To enter the legend.

Set up titles.

Select: **T F** .... Titles command for **First** title line.
Type: **QUARTERLY INCOME STATEMENT**
Press: **<Return>**.......... To enter the title.

Select: **T S** .... Titles command for **Second** title line.
Type: **YOUR NAME**
Press: **<Return>**.......... To enter the title.

Select: **T X** .... Titles command for **X**-axis.
Type: **1ST QUARTER, 1987**
Press: **<Return>**.......... To enter the title.

Select: **T Y** .... Titles command for **Y**-axis.
Type: **DOLLARS**
Press: **<Return>**.......... To enter the title.

Select: **Q** .... Quit the options.

Select: **V** .... View graph command.

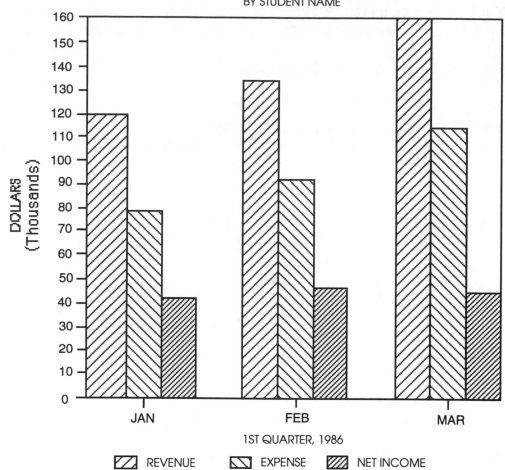

QUARTERLY INCOME STATEMENT
BY STUDENT NAME

1ST QUARTER, 1986

Press: Any key .... To return to graph commands.
Select: **Q** .... **Q**uit option; return to READY mode.

Save your graph settings with the worksheet.
Select: **/ F S**   Press: **<Return>**   Select: **R**

Other Graphing Features

When in the READY mode, pressing the **<F10>** function key will display the current graph. If you make a change to any of the cells that are in the ranges you graphed, the graph will be electronically updated. Try it! Change MAR Revenue (cell D5) to 170,000 and then press **<F10>** to view the updated graph. Change it back to 160,000 and press **<F10>** again.

Name:_____ Class:_____ Date:_____

File: **QIS**   Title: **Quarterly Income Statement**

[**Analyze**] **your solutions.**

VERIFY YOUR WORK. Compare your electronic and manual solutions.

(1) What is the total net income for the quarter? $_____.

(2) What is the total profit percentage for the quarter? _____%.

PREDICT RESULTS. Without using the computer, answer these questions.

(3) If February's expense is decreased by $5,000, total net income would be $_____ and
the total profit percentage would _____(increase/decrease).

PERFORM "WHAT-IF" ANALYSIS. Using the computer, confirm your predictions and
then answer the questions below.

(4) If January expense is $95,000, then:
Total profit percentage is _____%.
January profit percentage is _____%.
March profit percentage is _____%.

(5) Approximately how much revenue for March is needed to produce a 35% profit percentage for
March? $_____.
(Experiment with different amounts for March revenue until you narrow it down.)
At this point, what is the net income for March? $_____.

Chapter Contents

This chapter consists of six problem applications. The first five are partially set up in a template format on the *Computer Resource Guide* disk (*CRG* disk) with the file names as shown. You will create the last problem (installment sales), starting with a blank worksheet. The page numbers are shown for the problem and for the analysis sheet, which is found at the back of the manual.

File	Topic	Problem	Analysis
BAN	Bank Reconciliation	120	201
REC	Accounts Receivable Credit Losses	122	203
LCM	Inventory - Lower of Cost or Market	124	205
DEP	Depreciation	126	207
PAY	Payroll Accounting	128	209
INS	Installment Sales	130	211

Suggested Procedures

You will be asked to solve each problem manually, writing your answers directly on the worksheet provided. You will then establish the relationships between data elements by writing your formulas and functions directly on the form provided. Next, using the appropriate file name, you will retrieve the template file from the disk and proceed to complete the formulas as needed and process your data inputs. Formulas are needed in each cell that displays the word "FORMULA." A problem analysis sheet will give you an opportunity to electronically experiment with your program using a "what-if" approach. Finally, some problems will have an alternative problem with a different set of data inputs. Try using your programmed spreadsheet to solve these problems.

Suggestion

Try using the "point and pick" method of selecting the file. After selecting **/ F R** (the file retrieve command), use the arrow keys to point to the file name that is shown on the third line of the control panel, and then press the **<Return>** key to pick the highlighted file. If the file you want to pick is not displayed on the third line of the control panel, press the **<Down>** arrow key to display the next group of files.

Solve the problem manually.

On July 31, Sullivan Company's Cash in Bank account had a balance of $7,216.60. On that date, the bank statement indicated a balance of $9,534.75. Comparison of returned checks and bank advices revealed the following:

(1) Deposits in transit July 31 amounted to $3,140.75.
(2) Outstanding checks July 31 totaled $1,467.90.
(3) The bank erroneously charged a $325 check of the Solloman Company against the Sullivan bank account.
(4) A $25 bank service charge has not yet been recorded on the books.
(5) Sullivan neglected to record $4,000 borrowed from the bank on a 10%, six-month note. The bank statement shows the $4,000 as a deposit.
(6) Included with the returned checks is a memo indicating that J. Martin's check for $640 had been returned NSF. Martin, a customer, had sent the check to pay an account of $660 less $20 discount.
(7) Sullivan Company recorded a $109 payment for repairs as $1,090.

Complete the bank reconciliation worksheet for Sullivan Company at July 31 by writing your answers directly in the appropriate boxes below.

	A	B	C	D	E
1	Preparer's Name:				
2	Spreadsheet Title: Sullivan Company, Bank Reconciliation				
3	Date:				
4		BANK			BOOKS
5	Balance per bank			Balance per books	
6	Add:			Add:	
7	Deposits in transit			Bank credits	
8	Other			Other	
9	Other			Other	
10					
11	Subtract:			Subtract:	
12	Outstanding checks			Bank charges	
13	Other			Other	
14	Other			Other	
15					
16					
17	Adjusted bank balance			Adjusted book balance	
18					
19	Unreconciled difference				

Program the relationships.

Cell Description	Cell	Primary Formula	Copy To
Adjusted Bank Balance	B17	@SUM( )	E17
Unreconciled Difference	B19		

| **Create** | the electronic worksheet.

☐ Retrieve the template file **BAN**. The input cells should be displayed in higher intensity. You may have to adjust the brightness or contrast knobs on the monitor. Enter your name and other identification in cell B1.

☐ Use the "point" method to enter the formula in cell B17.

Move:	**B17**......................	Adjusted bank balance
Type:	**@SUM(**	Enter first part of the function.
Press:	**<Up>** 3 times	Move up to cell B14.
Type:	**.**	Type a period to anchor cell B14 as the beginning range.
Press:	**<Up>** 9 times	To move up to cell B5, highlighting the cells to add.
Type:	**)**	Type the right parenthesis to complete the function.
Press:	**<Return>**	To enter the function.

☐ Copy the primary formula to cell E17.

Move:	**B17**......................	Adjusted bank balance
Select:	**/ C**	Copy command.
Press:	**<Return>**.............	To enter cell B17 as the FROM cell.
Press:	**<Right>** 3 times	To move to cell E17 and begin the TO range.
Press:	**<Return>**	To end the TO range and complete the command.

☐ Enter the formula for the unreconciled difference.

Move:	**B19**......................	Unreconciled difference.
Type:	**+**........................	Enter a plus sign to begin the formula.
Move:	**E17**......................	To enter the adjusted book balance into the formula.
Type:	**-**	Enter a minus sign as the next operator.
Move:	**B17**......................	To enter the adjusted book balance into the formula.
Press:	**<Return>**.............	To enter and complete the formula.

Your worksheet should show zeros for the three amounts. The cells have been formatted to display dollars and cents. Notice that you have completed your program without typing any cell addresses. You will find this technique to be quick and easy. It might be a good idea to try it again, this time without looking at the instructions.

☐ Enter your data inputs to complete the problem. Remember to use the numbers at the top of the keyboard. Do not enter commas but do enter the decimal where cents are used. If the dollars are even and no cents are involved, you will not need to enter the decimal or the cents. Enter the items to be subtracted as negative numbers by typing a minus sign before the number.

☐ Save your work. When you are satisfied that your program is correct, save your worksheet by replacing the old file with your newly modified file. Use the same file name and remember to select the **Replace** option as follows: **/ F S <Return> R**

☐ Use the analysis sheet to experiment with your worksheet. The analysis sheets are located at the back of this manual.

Solve the problem manually.

At December 31, 1993 Schuler Company had a balance of $360,000 in its Accounts Receivable account and a credit balance of $4,200 in the Allowance for Uncollectible Accounts account. The accounts receivable subsidiary ledger consisted of $365,000 in debit balances and $5,000 in credit balances. The company bases its provision for credit losses on the aging analysis. Complete the worksheet manually.

	A	B	C	D	E
1	Preparer's Name:				
2	Spreadsheet Title:	Schuler Company			
3	Date:	December 31, 1993			
4	Accounts Receivable	Balance	Pct	Est Loss	Net Amount
5	Current	304,000	1.00%		
6	0-60 days past due	34,000	5.00%		
7	61-180 days past due	18,000	15.00%		
8	Over 6 months past due	9,000	40.00%		
9					
10	Balance Sheet Totals				
11					
12	Total Expected Loss				
13	Allowance Balance	4,200			
14	Expense Provision				

Program the relationships.

Cell Description	Cell	Primary Formulas	Copy To
Current Est Loss	D5		D6..D8
Current Net Amount	E5		E6..E8
Balance Sheet totals	B10		D10..E10
Total Expected Loss	B12		
Expense Provision	B14		

Create the electronic worksheet.

❏ Retrieve the template file **REC**. The input cells should be displayed in higher intensity. You may have to adjust the brightness or contrast knobs on the monitor. Enter your name and other identification in cell B1.

❏ Enter the formula for cell D5. Move to cell D5 and type a plus sign (the large key to the right of the **<PgDn>** key) to begin the formula. Use the arrow keys to point to the first cell in your formula. Type an asterisk (the key to the left of the **<End>** key) to indicate multiplication and then point to the next cell in the formula. Finally, press the **<Return>** key to enter the formula.

❏ Copy the formula in cell D5 to cells D6 through D8 as follows:

Move:	**D5**	You should still be there after the prior step.
Select:	**/ C**	Copy command.
Press:	**<Return>**	To enter cell D5 as the FROM cell.
Press:	**<Down>**	To move to cell D6.
Type:	**.**	Enter a period to anchor cell D6.
Press:	**<Down>** 2 times	To highlight copy TO range.
Press:	**<Return>**	To end the TO range and complete the command.

❏ Enter the formula for cell E5.

❏ Copy the formula in cell E5 to cells E6 through E8.

❏ Enter the formulas for the totals in row 10; use the @SUM function.

❏ Enter the formula for the total expected loss. Actually, this amount has already been calculated in cell D10. You could enter the same formula, but it is much easier just to refer to cell D10 as follows:

Move:	**B12**
Type:	**+**
Move:	**D10**
Press:	**<Return>**

❏ Enter the formula for the Expense Provision.

❏ Save your work. When you are satisfied that your program is correct, save your worksheet by replacing the old file with your newly modified file. Use the same file name and remember to select the **R**eplace option.

❏ Complete the analysis sheet.

Solve the problem manually.

Venner Company had the following inventory at December 31, 1993. Determine the ending inventory amount by applying the lower of cost or market rule using the three methods shown at the bottom of the worksheet.

	A	B	C	D	E	F	G
1	Preparer's Name:						
2	Spreadsheet Title: Venner Company, Inventory - Lower of Cost or Market						
3			Unit	Unit	Total	Total	Lower
4	Fans		Cost	Market	Cost	Market	Cost/Mkt
5	Model X1	300	18	19			
6	Model X2	250	22	24			
7	Model X3	400	29	26			
8	Total Fans						
9	Heaters						
10	Model B7	500	24	28			
11	Model B8	290	35	32			
12	Model B9	100	40	38			
13	Total Heaters						
14							
15	Grand Total						
16							
17	Inventory by each item						
18	Inventory by each category						
19	Inventory by grand total						

Program the relationships.

Cell Description	Cell	Primary Formulas	Copy To
Total Cost Model X1	E5		E6..E7
Total Market Model X1	F5		F6..F7
Lower Cost/Mkt Model x1	G5	@MIN( )	G6..G7
Total Cost, Fans	E8	@SUM( )	F8

Total Cost, Grand Total	E15		F15
By each item	E17	@SUM( )	
By each category	E18	@MIN( )+	
		@MIN( )	
By grand total	E19	@MIN( )	

Create the electronic worksheet.

❏ Retrieve the template file **LCM**.

❏ Using your worksheet skills, enter the formulas for the inventory of fans. The **@MIN** function will determine the minimum value of a range of cells and takes the form **@MIN(E5..F5)** where E5 is the first cell and F5 is the last cell in the range. You can enter the **@MIN** function just like you would enter the **@SUM** function. The difference is that the **@MIN** function will determine the minimum value in a range and the **@SUM** function will determine the total value of cells in a range.

❏ Enter the formulas for heaters by copying the formulas for fans. Usually you will copy only one formula to a group of related cells. In this problem you will copy a range of formulas (fans) to another range (heaters).

Move:	**E5**	
Select:	**/ C**....................	Copy command.
Press:	**Arrow Keys**.........	To highlight the range E5 through G8 (Fans).
Press:	**<Return>**..............	To complete copy FROM range.
Move:	**E10**......................	First copy TO cell.
Press:	**<Return>**.............	To end the TO range and complete the command.

❏ Enter the rest of the formulas. In cell E18, the inventory by each item requires you to add the minimum of the total of the fans to the minimum of the total of the heaters.

❏ Save your work. When you are satisfied that your program is correct, save your worksheet by replacing the old file with your newly modified file. Use the same file name and remember to select the **R**eplace option.

❏ Complete the analysis sheet.

Solve the problem manually.

On January 2, Roth, Inc. purchased a laser cutting machine to be used in the fabrication of a part for one of its key products. The machine cost $72,000, and its estimated useful life was four years, after which it could be sold for $4,500. Calculate the depreciation expense, accumulated depreciation, and book value for the life of the machine using the straight line and double declining balance methods. Write your answers in the appropriate boxes below.

	A	B	C	D	E	F	G	H
1	Preparer's Name:							
2	Spreadsheet Title: Roth, Inc., Depreciation							
3								
4	Machine cost		72,000	SL Rate				
5	Salvage value		4,500	DDB Rate				
6	Est life in years		4					
7	------------------ STRAIGHT LINE ------------------				----------- DOUBLE DECLINING BAL ---------			
8		Depreciation	Accumulated	Book		Depreciation	Accumulated	Book
9	Year	Expense	Depreciation	Value		Expense	Depreciation	Value
10	1							
11	2							
12	3							
13	4							
14	5							
15	6							
16	7							
17	8							
18	9							
19	10							
20	Total							

Program the relationships.

Years 2 through 10 and the totals have been preprogrammed. Enter your formulas for the depreciation rates and for Year 1.

Cell Description	Cell	Primary Formulas
SL Rate	F4	
DDB Rate	F5	

Straight Line		
Depreciation Expense	B10	
Accum Depreciation	C10	
Book Value	D10	

Double Declining		
Depreciation Expense	F10	
Accum Depreciation	G10	
Book Value	H10	

| Create | the electronic worksheet.

□ Retrieve the template file **DEP**. This file has been partially programmed and protected. The input cells and certain formula cells have been unprotected, allowing you to make the necessary changes.

□ Enter the three data inputs for cost, salvage, and estimated life in column C.

□ Enter the formulas for the straight line and double declining depreciation rates. The double declining rate is twice the straight line rate.

□ Enter the first year formulas for both straight line and double declining methods.

□ Years 2 through 10 and the totals have been preprogrammed to provide flexibility for different depreciation lives, up to a maximum of 10 years. These formulas involve the **@IF** function, which first checks to see if the current year is greater than the estimated life. If it is, then depreciation expense is zero. If not, then the depreciation is calculated. Your formulas for the first year do not need to use the @IF function. The formula for straight line depreciation in cell B11 is:

> **@IF(A11>$C$6,0,($C$4-$C$5)/$C$6)**

Within the parentheses there are three separate parts separated by commas.

Part one **A11>$C$6** This is the condition to check.
Part two **0** This is the answer if the condition is true (enter a zero in the cell).
Part three **($C$4-$C$5)/$C$6** This is the answer if the condition is false.

The dollar signs are used to make a cell an absolute reference, which allows the formula to be copied. Move the pointer to cell B12 and then B13. You will see that the formula is the same except for the current year (cell A11), which is a relative reference.

□ When you are satisfied that your worksheet is correct, save your work.

□ Complete the analysis sheet.

Solve the problem manually.

Edgewater Company employs five persons, all of whom are paid an hourly rate. All employees receive overtime pay at one and a half times their regular pay rate. FICA tax is 7.65% of gross earnings. Using the information given, complete the worksheet filling in the empty boxes.

	A	B	C	D	E	F
1	Preparer's Name:					
2	Spreadsheet Title: Edgewater Company, Payroll					
3	Date: Week ended March 31, 1993					
4		Regular	Overtime	Gross		
5		Earnings	Earnings	Earnings		
6	James Allen					
7	Paul Durango					
8	Ann Poole					
9	John Scott					
10	Amy Thorp					
11	Totals					
12						
13		D e d u c t i o n s				Net
14		FICA Tax	Fed Inc Tax	Medical	Total	Earnings
15	James Allen		60.00	5.00		
16	Paul Durango		75.00	5.00		
17	Ann Poole		36.00	5.00		
18	John Scott		31.00	5.00		
19	Amy Thorp		24.00	5.00		
20	Totals					
21						
22						
23		Pay Rate	Hours	Overtime		
24	Employee	Per Hour	Worked	Hours		
25	James Allen	9.00	44	4		
26	Paul Durango	12.00	40	0		
27	Ann Poole	8.00	42	2		
28	John Scott	9.00	40	0		
29	Amy Thorp	8.00	40	0		

Program the relationships.

This problem has been partially preprogrammed. You will be asked to program the gross earnings and the net earnings only. In the next step you will retrieve the programmed template and process the data inputs, which are given in the problem above.

Create the electronic worksheet.

❐ Retrieve the template file **PAY**. This problem has been preprogrammed except for the gross earnings and the net earnings. One approach to entering these formulas might be to enter the formula for gross earnings for James Allen and then copy it for the other employees. Also, there is a primary formula in cell C11 that could be copied to D11 rather than entering another formula. Try it! This same approach will work for the net earnings.

❐ Save your work.

Solve the problem manually.

During December 1993, Gator Realty Company sold several residential lots on an installment basis. The sales totaled $400,000. Terms were 30% down on the date of purchase and 20 equal monthly payments beginning January 2, 1994. The cost of property sold on the installment basis was $232,000. Gator Realty Company elects the installment method to report the gross profit from these sales on its income tax return.

	A	B	C	D	E
1	Preparer's Name:				
2	Spreadsheet Title: Gator Realty Company, Installment Sales				
3	Date: December 1993				
4					
5			Scheduled Cash Collections		
6		Total	1993	1994	1995
7	Sales	400,000	120,000	168,000	112,000
8	Cost of property sold	232,000			
9	Gross profit				
10					
11	Gross profit percent				

Program the relationships.

Cell Description	Cell	Primary Formula	Copy To
Gross profit	B9		
Gross profit percent	B11		
1993 Gross profit percent	C11		D11..E11
1993 Gross profit	C9		D9..E9
1993 Cost of goods sold	C8		D8..E8

❑ This problem does not have a template file on the floppy disk. You will start with a blank worksheet and enter all labels and values. If necessary, refer to the sample problems in Chapter 9 for assistance. When you have completed your worksheet, save it using the file name **INS**.

❑ Begin with a blank worksheet and then enter the labels and the numeric inputs as shown. You will need to widen column A and format the appropriate labels. Again, refer to Chapter 9 if necessary. You can wait to format the numbers until after the worksheet is programmed.

❑ Enter the formulas for the total gross profit and gross profit percent. Hopefully you will do this without using your hand written formulas and by pointing to the appropriate cell locations.

❑ Enter the formula for the 1993 gross profit percent. Because the percent is the same for all years, you can use the formula **+B11** to refer to cell B11. This can be copied to cells D11 and E11. Because copying is relative, notice that the formula in cell D11 now refers to cell C11, and the formula in cell E11 refers to cell D11. In other words, the relative formula in cells C11, D11, and E11 is "use the value in the cell to the left."

❑ Next, enter your formula for 1993 gross profit and cost of property sold, and then copy these to the years 1994 and 1995.

❑ Dress up, protect, and save your worksheet using the file name **INS**. Refer to Chapter 9 if necessary.

❑ If your computer is equipped to display graphics, try graphing some of the relationships.

❑ Complete the analysis sheet.

CHAPTER 11 ■ SPREADSHEETS: Partnerships and Corporations

Chapter Contents

This chapter consists of six problem applications that are partially set up in template format on the *Computer Resource Guide* disk (*CRG* disk). Each application is represented on the disk by an electronic file with the names as shown. The page numbers are shown for the problem and for the analysis sheet that is found at the back of the manual.

Suggested Procedures

You will be asked to solve each problem manually, writing your answers directly on the worksheet provided. You will then establish the relationships between data elements, writing your formulas and functions directly on the form provided. Next, using the appropriate file name, you will retrieve the template file from the disk and proceed to complete the formulas as needed and process your data inputs. Formulas are needed in each cell that displays the word "FORMULA." A problem analysis sheet will give you an opportunity to electronically experiment with your program using a "what-if" approach. Finally, some problems will have an alternative problem with a different set of data inputs. Try using your programmed spreadsheet to solve these problems.

Suggestion

> Try using the "point and pick" method of selecting the file. After selecting **/ F R** (the file retrieve command), use the arrow keys to point to the file name that is shown on the third line of the control panel, and then press the **<Return>** key to pick the highlighted file. If the file you want to pick is not displayed on the third line of the control panel, press the **<Down>** arrow key to display the next group of files.

Solve the problem manually.

The capital accounts and the income allocation for Dole, Fine, and Thomas partnership appear below. None of the partners withdrew capital during the year. Complete the worksheet to distribute the $120,000 net income with the assumptions as shown.

	A	B	C	D	E
1	Preparer's Name:				
2	Spreadsheet Title:	Partnership Income Allocation			
3					
4	Profit & Loss Ratio		50.00%	30.00%	20.00%
5					
6		TOTAL	Dole	Fine	Thomas
7	Net Income (Loss)	120,000			
8	Salary Allowance		0	0	20,000
9	Interest Allowance		4,800	6,400	16,000
10	Other Allowance		0	0	0
11	Residual Income (Loss)				
12					
13					
14	Beginning Capital		48,000	64,000	160,000
15	Contributions		64,000	64,000	0
16	Drawings		0	0	0
17	Net Income (Loss)				
18	Ending Capital				

Program the relationships.

Cell Description	Cell	Primary Formulas	Copy To
Profit & Loss Ratio	B4		
Salary Allowance	B8		B9..B10
Residual Income (Loss)	B11		
Residual Income (Loss) Read	C11	+ C4 * $B$11	D11..E11
Total Net Income	C7	@SUM( )	D7..E7
Net Income (Loss), Read	C17		D17..E17
Beginning Capital	B14	@SUM( )	B15..B17
Ending Capital	B18	@SUM( )	C18..E18

Create the electronic worksheet.

☐ Retrieve the template file **PAR**. The input cells should be displayed in higher intensity. You may have to adjust the brightness or contrast knobs on the monitor. Enter your name and other identification in cell B1.

☐ Enter the formula for the total profit & loss ratio in cell B4. Enter the formula for the total salary allowance (cell B8) and copy this for the total interest allowances and other allowances (cells B9 and B10).

☐ Enter the formula for the residual income (loss) in cell B11. The residual income (loss) is determined by subtracting the allowances from the original net income (loss) in cell B7. The original net income (loss) is before any allowances to the individual partners.

☐ Allocate the total residual income (loss) in cell B11 to the individual partners according to the profit & loss ratio. You could enter the following three formulas:

Cell	Formula
C11	C4 * B11
D11	D4 * B11
E11	E4 * B11

Notice that the references to cell B11 are the same in all three formulas. This is called an <u>absolute reference</u>. The references to cells C4, D4, and E4 are relative references because the columns change but the rows do not.

Part of each formula is absolute and part is relative. If you want to enter the formula once and then copy it, you must make the reference to cell B11 absolute by placing a dollar sign before the column and the row (**$B$11**). This can be accomplished either by typing the dollar signs or by using the absolute function key **<F4>.**

Let's enter the formula using the function key.

Move:	**C11**.....................	The first partner's share of the residual income.
Type:	**+**	To begin the formula.
Move:	**C4**......................	To include the first cell.
Type:	*****	The multiplication operator (asterisk).
Move:	**B11**.....................	To include the next cell.
Press:	**<F4>**	The absolute function key makes cell B11 absolute.
Press:	**<Return>**..............	To complete the formula.

Now you can copy the formula in cell C11 to cells D11 and E11, and the reference to cell B11 will stay the same without shifting columns.

☐ Enter the formula for each partner's share of the original net income (loss) by adding the allowances and residual net income (loss) for each partner.

☐ Program the partners' capital summary at the bottom of the worksheet. Although the net income (loss) has already been calculated in row 7, you cannot copy this formula to row 17 but you can refer to the value by entering in cell C17 the formula **+C7**. This can then be copied to cells D7 and E7.

☐ Save your work and use the analysis sheet to experiment with your worksheet.

Solve the problem manually.

The Rydon Corporation has outstanding 30,000 shares of $100 par value, 7%, cumulative preferred stock and 100,000 shares of $10 par value common stock. The company has declared cash dividends of $760,000. Assuming that preferred stock is nonparticipating and one year's dividend arrearage exists on the preferred stock, complete the worksheet by filling in the boxes.

	A	B	C	D
1	Preparer's Name:			
2	Spreadsheet Title: Rydon Corporation, Cash Dividends			
3				
4		Total	Preferred	Common
5	Preferred - Current	210,006	210,000	
6	Preferred - In arrears	210,060	210,000	
7	Preferred - Participating	0	0	
8	Common - Balance	340,000		340,060
9				
10	Total Cash Dividends	760,000	420,000	340,000
11				
12	Shares outstanding		30,000	100,000
13				
14	Dividends per share		14	3.4

Program the relationships.

Cell Description	Cell	Primary Formulas	Copy To
Preferred - Current	B5	@Sum(C5..95)	B6..B7
Common - Balance	B8	@Sum(C8..D8)	
Common - Balance	D8	+B10-C10	
Total Cash Dividends	C10	@SUM(C5..C8)	D10
Dividends per share	C14	+C10/C12	D14

Create the electronic worksheet.

❏ Retrieve the template file **DIV**. The input cells should be displayed in higher intensity. Enter your name and other identification in cell B1.

❏ Using your worksheet skills, enter the formulas.

❏ Save your work. When you are satisfied that your program is correct, save your worksheet by replacing the old file with your newly modified file. Use the same file name and remember to select the **R**eplace option.

❏ Complete the analysis sheet.

760

[Solve] **the problem manually.**

Bowden Corporation discloses earnings per share amounts for extraordinary items and reports extraordinary items net of income tax.
Complete the worksheet below, writing your answers in the appropriate boxes.
Write the formulas in the boxes at the far right.

	A	B	C	D	
1	Preparer's Name:				
2	Spreadsheet Title: Bowden Corporation, Income Statement				
3	Date: Year Ended December 31, 1993				
4					
5	Sales			990,000	
6	Cost of goods sold			600,000	Formulas
7	Gross profit on sales			☐	☐
8	Less: Selling expenses		77,000		
9	Administrative expenses		95,000		
10	Loss on sale of equipment		8,000	☐	☐
11	NI before taxes & extraord. item			☐	☐
12	Less: Income taxes	40%		☐	☐
13	Income before extraord. item			☐	☐
14	Extraordinary loss item	55,000		☐	☐
15	Net income			☐	☐
16					
17	Earnings per share of common stock:				
18	Income before extraordinary item			☐	☐
19	Extraordinary loss (net of tax)			☐	☐
20	Net income		PgDn	☐	☐
21			PgUp		
22					
23		Weighted average of common shares:			
24			Issued	Balance	
25		Beginning		27,000	Formulas
26		January	0	☐	☐
27		February	0	☐	
28		March	0	☐	
29		April	0	☐	
30		May	4,000	☐	
31		June	0	☐	Copy
32		July	0	☐	formula
33		August	0	☐	
34		September	0	☐	
35		October	0	☐	
36		November	2,000	☐	
37		December	0	☐	
38		Totals		☐	☐
39		Average		☐	☐
40					

> **Create** the electronic worksheet.

❑ Retrieve the template file **EPS**. If necessary, adjust the brightness to show the inputs at higher intensity and enter your name and identification.

❑ Enter the formulas for the income statement section in the top window. When programming the earnings per share section, you will need to refer to the bottom window for the average of the common shares. If you are entering your formulas by the "pointing" method, you can point to cell D39 by pressing the **<PgDn>** key to flip to the bottom window and then moving to cell D39 using the arrow keys. When you press the **<Return>** key to enter the formula, 1-2-3 will automatically return to the formula cell in the top window. Also, if you program the earnings per share section before programming the average of common shares (cell D39), the result of your formula will be displayed as **ERR**, meaning that you are dividing by zero (which is not allowed). This will be automatically changed after you program the average in the bottom window.

❑ Enter the formula for the balance of outstanding shares for January and then copy this formula for the rest of the months. The formula for the balance of any month is the prior balance plus the shares issued during the month.

❑ Enter the formula for the totals of the monthly balances (cells D26 through D37). Do not include the beginning balance in cell D25.

❑ Enter the formula for the average. There are two ways to do this: divide the totals in cell D38 by 12, or use the average function **@AVG**. Here's how you could use the function:

Move:	**D39**	Average shares.
Type:	**@AVG(**	Enter first part of the function.
Press:	**<Up>** 2 times..........	Move up to cell D37.
Type:	**.**	Type a period to anchor cell D37 as the beginning range.
Press:	**<Up>** 11 times	To move up to cell D26, highlighting the cells to average.
Type:	**)**	Type the right parenthesis to complete the function.
Press:	**<Return>**	To enter the function.

❑ Save your work. When you are satisfied that your program is correct, save your worksheet by replacing the old file with your newly modified file. Use the same file name and remember to select the **Replace** option.

❑ Complete the analysis sheet.

Solve the problem manually.

On December 31, 1993, Caper, Inc. issued $600,000 face value, 8%, 10-year bonds for $525,288, yielding an effective interest rate of 10%. Semiannual interest is payable on June 30 and December 31 each year. The firm uses the effective interest method to amortize the discount. Manually complete the worksheet for the first two years.

	A	B	C	D	E	F
1	Preparer's Name:					
2	Spreadsheet Title: Caper Inc., Bonds Payable					
3						
4	Bond Contract					
5	Bond face amount	600,000	Bond sales price		525,288	
6	Interest rate	8.00%	Market interest rate		10.00%	
7	Term in years	10	Bond premium (discount)			
8						
9	Year / Period	Interest Paid	Interest Exp	Amortization	Balance	Book Value
10	Beginning Balances					
11	Year 1 / Period 1					
12	Year 1 / Period 2					
13	Year 2 / Period 3					
14	Year 2 / Period 4					

This problem has been preprogrammed, allowing only the data inputs to be changed. Turn to the next page and process the data inputs.

⬛ **Process** the data inputs.

☐ Retrieve the template file **BON**. The worksheet has been protected, allowing only the data inputs to be changed.

☐ Enter the three data inputs for the bond contract. Also enter the bond sales price and the market interest rate.

☐ After entering the inputs, press the **<PgDn>** key to see the remainder of the amortization schedule. In the case of bonds selling at a discount, the book value increases each period as the discount is amortized. At the end of the bond life, the discount account will be fully amortized, leaving a book value equal to the face amount of the bonds payable. Using the data inputs given in the problem, the discount account is slightly over amortized at the end of the bond life. This would be adjusted in the last period by making the amortization equal to the balance in the discount account.

☐ 1-2-3 has the ability to split the worksheet window into two windows, horizontally or vertically. Let's split the window horizontally so that the data inputs and the bottom of the amortization schedule are both visible at the same time.

Move:	**A11**.....................	The top of the second window.
Select:	**/ W W**..................	**W**orksheet **W**indow command.
Select:	**H**.........................	**H**orizontal option.
Press:	**<F6>**....................	Window function key to jump to the other window.
Press:	**<PgDn>** 2 times....	To move to the bottom of the schedule.
Press:	**<Up>** 5 times	To adjust bottom window view.
Press:	**<F6>**....................	To jump back to the top window.

With both windows in view, change the market interest rate to 9%. You will notice that the discount balance does not decrease with amortization but increases. This indicates that for a market rate of 9%, the discount is too high or the selling price of $525,288 is too low. Try increasing the selling price to $550,000. By experimenting with the selling price, you could find the approximate selling price for the 9% market interest rate.

To clear the second window:
Select:	**/ W W C**...............	**W**orksheet **W**indow **C**lear command.

☐ Complete the analysis sheet.

Solve the problem manually.

On January 1, 1994, Katt Company purchased 85% of the common stock of Harbor Company for $490,000 cash, after which the separate balance sheets of the two firms were as shown in the worksheet. Complete the worksheet by filling in the appropriate boxes including the eliminating entry.

	A	B	C	D	E	F
					Eliminations	
1	Preparer's Name:					
2	Spreadsheet Title:	Katt and Harbor Companies, Consolidated Balance Sheet				
3	Date:	January 1, 1994				
4					Eliminations	
5	ASSETS	Katt	Harbor	Debit	Credit	Total
6	Investment in Harbor	490,000				
7	Other Assets	1,210,000	600,000			
8	Goodwill					
9	Total Assets					
10						
11	EQUITIES					
12	Liabilities	310,000	100,000			
13	Common Stock	1,000,000	380,000			
14	Retained Earnings	390,000	120,000			
15	Minority Interest					
16	Total Equities					

Program the relationships.

Cell Description	Cell	Primary Formulas	Copy To
Total Assets	B9		C9 and F9
Total Equities	B16		C16 and F16
Total Debits	D16		E16
Total Investment	F6		F7..F8
Total Liabilities	F12		F13..F15

Create the electronic worksheet.

❏ Retrieve the template file **CBS**.

❏ Using your worksheet skills, enter the formulas.

❏ After you have programmed the worksheet, enter the eliminating worksheet entries. After each debit or credit amount is entered, the worksheet will be instantly updated.

❏ Save your work. When you are satisfied that your program is correct, save your worksheet by replacing the old file with your newly modified file. Use the same file name and remember to select the **R**eplace option.

❏ Complete the analysis sheet.

Solve the problem manually.

Consider the following income statement for the Waverly Company for 1993 and 1994. During 1994, management obtained additional bond financing to enlarge its production facilities. The company faced higher production costs during the year for such things as fuel, materials, and freight. Because of temporary government price controls, a planned price increase on products was delayed several months. Complete the worksheet as part of your analysis.

	A	B	C	D	E	F	G
1	Preparer's Name:						
2	Spreadsheet Title: Waverly Company, Income Statement Analysis						
3							
4						Increase	
5		Dec 1994	Pct%	Dec 1993	Pct%	(Decrease)	Pct%
6	Net Sales	810,000		675,000			
7	Cost of Goods Sold	526,500		425,250			
8	Gross Profit	283,500		249,750			
9	Selling & Admin Expenses	173,400		150,100			
10	Operating Income	110,100		99,650			
11	Bond Interest Expense	22,500		15,000			
12	Income before Taxes	87,600		84,650			
13	Income Tax Expense	23,250		22,450			
14	Net Income	64,350		62,200			

Program the relationships.

Cell Description	Cell	Primary Formulas	Copy To
Net Sales Pct% 94	C6	+ B6 / $B$6	C7..C14
Net Sales Pct% 93	E6	+E6/$E$6	E7..E14
Net Sales Increase	F6	+B6 - D6	F7..F14
Net Sales Pct%	G6	+F6/D6	G7..G14

❏ Retrieve the template file **ISA**. The input cells should be displayed in higher intensity. You may have to adjust the brightness or contrast knobs on the monitor. Enter your name and other identification in cell B1.

❏ The template file requires 36 formulas. If you had to type each of these formulas, you would probably turn to the next problem at this point. There are only four primary formulas, each of which can be easily entered by pointing to the appropriate cell references. Each of the two primary percentage formulas (cells C6 and E6) contains an absolute reference. Absolute references were introduced in the partnership problem in Chapter 11 (template file **PAR**). Let's review absolute references by looking at the formulas in column C.

	Pct% 1994
Net Sales	+B6/B6
Cost of Goods Sold	+B7/B6
Gross Profit	+B8/B6
Selling & Adm Expense	+B9/B6
Operating Income	+B10/B6
Bond Interest Expense	+B11/B6
Income before Taxes	+B12/B6
Income Tax Expense	+B13/B6
Net Income	+B14/B6

Notice that the reference to cell B6 is the same in all nine formulas. This is called an <u>absolute reference</u>. The references to cells B6.. B14 are relative references because the rows change but the columns do not. Part of each formula is absolute and part is relative. If you want to enter the formula once and then copy it, you must make the reference to cell B6 absolute by placing a dollar sign before the column and the row (**$B$6**). This can be accomplished either by typing the dollar signs or by using the absolute function key **<F4>**.

Let's enter the formula using the function key.

Move:	**C6**	The net sales percent.
Type:	**+**	To begin the formula.
Move:	**B6**	To include the first cell.
Type:	**/**	The division operator (Slash key).
Move:	**B6**	To include the next cell.
Press:	**<F4>**	To make the reference to cell B6 absolute.
Press:	**<Return>**	To complete the formula.

Now you can copy the formula in cell C6 to cells C7..C14 and the reference to cell B6 will stay the same without shifting rows.

❏ Enter the formula for cell E6 using the absolute function as demonstrated above. Copy this formula to other cells for column E.

❏ Enter the formula for the dollar increase/decrease in cell F6 (subtract 1993 from 1994) and copy this formula to other cells for column F. All references are relative.

❏ Enter the formula for the percent of the increase/decrease in column G using the amounts in column D as the base (divide the dollar change by 1993 amounts). Copy this formula as indicated.

❏ Save your work and use the analysis sheet to experiment with your worksheet.

Chapter Contents

This chapter consists of six problem applications that are partially set up in a template format on the *Computer Resource Guide* disk (*CRG* disk). Each application is represented on the disk by an electronic file with the names as shown. The page numbers are shown for the problem and for the analysis sheet, which is found at the back of the manual.

File	Topic	Problem	Analysis
MFG	Manufacturing Costs	148	225
PRO	Process Cost Accounting	150	227
CVP	Cost-Volume-Profit Relationships	152	229
AVC	Absorption/Variable Costing	154	231
VAR	Standard Costs and Variances	156	233
CAP	Capital Budgeting	158	235

Suggested Procedures

You will be asked to solve each problem manually, writing your answers directly on the worksheet provided. You will then establish the relationships between data elements writing your formulas and functions directly on the form provided. Next, using the appropriate file name, you will retrieve the template file from the disk and proceed to complete the formulas as needed and process your data inputs. Formulas are needed in each cell that displays the word "FORMULA." A problem analysis sheet will give you an opportunity to electronically experiment with your program using a "what-if" approach. Finally, some problems will have an alternative problem with a different set of data inputs. Try using your programmed spreadsheet to solve these problems.

Suggestion

Try using the "point and pick" method of selecting the file. After selecting **/ F R** (the file retrieve command), use the arrow keys to point to the file name that is shown on the third line of the control panel, and then press the **<Return>** key to pick the highlighted file. If the file you want to pick is not displayed on the third line of the control panel, press the **<Down>** arrow key to display the next group of files.

File: **MFG**   Topic: **Manufacturing Costs**

Solve the problem manually.

The only product of Gregg Manufacturers, Inc. is produced in a continuous process. At the end of the current year, the ending inventories of work in process and finished goods were as shown below. Assuming that factory overhead is assigned at the rate of 80% of direct labor cost, compute the cost of the ending inventories and write your answers in the boxes below.

	A	B	C	D	E
1	Preparer's Name:				
2	Spreadsheet Title: Gregg Manufacturers, Inc., Manufacturing Costs				
3					
4		Cost Per Unit		Total Cost	
5		Work-In	Finished	Work-In	Finished
6		Progress	Goods	Progress	Goods
7	Direct Materials	8.00	10.00		
8	Direct Labor	9.00	12.00		
9	Factory Overhead				
10	Totals				
11					
12	Factory OH Rate	80.00%			
13	Total Units	5,000	7,000		

Program the relationships.

Cell Description	Cell	Primary Formulas	Copy To
Factory Overhead	B9		C9
Totals, WIP	B10		C10..E10
Direct Materials, WIP	D7		D8..D9
Direct Materials, FG	E7		E8..E9

Create the electronic worksheet.

☐ Retrieve the template file **MFG**. The input cells should be displayed in higher intensity. You may have to adjust the brightness or contrast knobs on the monitor. Enter your name and other identification in cell B1.

☐ Enter the formulas for per unit factory overhead in cells B9, and then copy to cell C9. Make the reference to cell B12 (factory overhead rate) an absolute reference.

    Move: **B9**
      Type: **+**........................ To begin the formula.
    Move: **B12**..................... Factory overhead rate.
    Press: **<F4>** .... To make reference to cell B12 absolute.
      Type: ***** .... Multiplication operator (asterisk).

Finish the formula.

You will find that using the function key **<F4>** is much easier than typing the dollar signs before the column and rows of the absolute cell.

☐ All references to the factory overhead rate and the total units should be absolute references. This will allow you to copy your formulas without shifting the reference point for these cells.

☐ Enter and copy the rest of your formulas.

☐ Dress up your worksheet with double and single underlines as well as dollar signs where appropriate. If necessary, refer to your sample problem in Chapter 9, step 7 (Quarterly Income Statement).

☐ Turn on the worksheet protection as shown in Chapter 9, step 10. The input cells have already been unprotected and are shown in higher intensity.

☐ Complete the analysis sheet.

| Solve | the problem manually.

Arrow Company processes a food seasoning powder through its Compounding Department and Packaging Department. In the Packaging Department, costs of direct material, direct labor, and factory overhead are incurred evenly throughout the process, and the combined cost input is included in the $78,260 conversion cost show below. The period cost input for materials of $93,000 represents the amount transferred in from the Compounding Department. The cost of the beginning inventory is $5,080.

	A	B	C	D	E	F
1	Preparer's Name:					
2	Spreadsheet Title: Arrow Company, August Production Report					
3			Percent To	Equivalent Units		
4		Total Units	Complete	Materials	Conversion	
5	Beginning inventory	2,000	60.00%			
6	Started and completed	28,000	100.00%			
7	Ending inventory	3,000	30.00%			
8	Total units					
9						
10	Period cost input			93,000	78,260	
11	Equivalent unit cost					
12						
13				Dollars		
14		Total Dollars		Materials	Conversion	
15	Beginning inventory			5,080		
16	Started and completed					
17	Transferred out					
18	Ending inventory					
19	Total dollars					
20						

| Program | the relationships.

The equivalent unit section has been preprogrammed. Program the formulas below:

Cell Description	Cell	Primary Formula	Copy To
Equivalent unit cost	D11		E11
Beginning inventory	E15		
Started and completed	D16		E16
Transferred out	D17	@SUM( )	E17
Ending inventory	D18		E18
Total dollars,materials	D19		E19
Beginning inventory	B15	@SUM( )	B16..B19

Create **the electronic worksheet.**

☐ Retrieve the template file **PRO**. You will notice that the equivalent units section has been preprogrammed.

☐ Program the equivalent unit costs.

☐ Program the bottom section of the worksheet. You will multiply the equivalent unit cost by the appropriate units in the section above. For example, the formula for cell E15 is the unit cost in cell E11 times the beginning inventory conversion units, cell E5.

☐ Save your work. When you are satisfied that your program is correct, save your worksheet by replacing the old file with your newly modified file. Use the same file name and remember to select the **Replace** option.

☐ Complete the analysis sheet.

Solve the problem manually.

Superior Corporation sells a single product for $60 per unit, of which $24 is variable cost and $36 is contribution margin. Total fixed costs are $72,000, and net income before tax is $28,800. Th number of actual units sold is determined by dividing the actual contribution margin (fixed costs plus net income) by the contribution margin per unit. Complete the worksheet by writing your answers directly in the boxes.

	A	B	C	D	E	F	G
1	Preparer's Name:						
2	Spreadsheet Title:	Superior Corporation, CVP Relationships					
3		Total	Percent				
4	Sales						
5	Less variable expenses				BE%	Sales	Net Income
6	Contribution margin				200%		
7	Less fixed expenses				175%		
8	Net income				150%		
9					125%		
10	Break-even sales		------->>		100%		
11	Break-even units				75%		
12					50%		
13	Independent Inputs				25%		
14	Unit sales price	60.00			0%		
15	Unit variable costs	24.00					
16	Total fixed costs	72,000					
17	Total unit sales	2,800					

Program the relationships.

Cell Description	Cell	Primary Formulas
Sales	B4	
Variable expense	B5	
Contribution margin	B6	
Fixed expenses	B7	
Net income	B8	

Break-even sales	B10	
Break-even units	B11	

Sales percent	C4	
Variable exp percent	C5	
Contribution ratio	C6	

Create the electronic worksheet.

☐ Retrieve the template file **CVP**.

☐ First, program the income statement for the actual level of sales as shown in the input section at the bottom of the worksheet. You should have a net income of $28,800 for sales of 2,800 units.

☐ Next, program the percentages in cells C4, C5, and C6.

☐ Program the break-even sales dollars and units.

☐ The table on the right side of the worksheet represents sales and net income for various percentages of break-even sales. The first level is 200% (double) the break-even sales level. Next is 175% of break-even sales, and so forth. This section has been preprogrammed and will be used in your analysis.

			Copy To
Sales	F6	+E6 * $B$10	F7..F14
Net income	G6	+F6 * $C$6 - $B$7	G7..G14

☐ When you are satisfied with your worksheet, protect your work and then save your worksheet. The input cells have already been unprotected. Turn on the worksheet protection by selecting **/ W G P E** (**W**orksheet **G**lobal **P**rotection **E**nable).

☐ Complete the analysis sheet.

⬚ **Solve** the problem manually.

Scott Manufacturing makes a product with total unit manufacturing costs of $54, of which $36 is variable. No units were on hand at the beginning of 1992. During 1992 and 1993, the only product manufactured was sold for $84 per unit, and the cost structure did not change. Scott uses the first-in, first-out inventory method and has the production and sales shown below. Complete the worksheet.

	A	B	C	D	E
1	Preparer's Name:				
2		ABSORPTION COSTING		VARIABLE COSTING	
3		1992 $	1993 $	1992 $	1993 $
4	Net sales				
5	Beginning inventory				
6	Cost of goods manufactured				
7	Goods available for sale				
8	Ending inventory				
9	Cost of goods sold				
10	Contribution Margin				
11	Less fixed costs				
12	Gross profit				
13					
14	Beginning units	0			
15	Units manufactured	120,000	120,000		
16	Units sold	90,000	130,000		
17	Ending units				
18	Unit manufacturing cost	54.00	54.00		
19	Unit variable mfg cost	36.00	36.00		
20	Unit sales price	84.00	84.00		

⬚ **Program** the relationships.

This problem has been partially preprogrammed. You will program the unit formulas shown below as well as selected formulas in the variable costing section.

Description	Cell	Primary Formula	Copy To
Ending units 1992	B17		C17
Beginning units 1993	C14		

⌐ Create ⌐ the electronic worksheet.

☐ Retrieve the template file **AVC**. You will notice that the absorption costing section has been preprogrammed. You will program the cells that display the word "FORMULA."

☐ First, program the unit formulas at the bottom of the worksheet.

☐ Next, program the variable cost section for all cells displaying the word "FORMULA." If necessary, look at the formulas for absorption costing to get programming ideas for variable costing. The basic difference between absorption and variable costing is that absorption costing uses the total unit manufacturing cost (including unit fixed cost) while variable costing uses only the unit variable manufacturing cost. Some of the formulas for Year 1993 are relative and can be copied from Year 1992, and some, such as the formula for beginning inventory, are not relative. The formula for the total fixed costs (cell D11) can be programmed as **(B18-B19)*B15**. The parentheses are required. Also, this is a relative formula for 1993.

☐ Save your work. When you are satisfied that your program is correct, save your worksheet by replacing the old file with your newly modified file. Use the same file name and remember to select the **R**eplace option.

☐ Complete the analysis sheet.

| Solve | the problem manually.

Milton Company has established unit standard costs for its only product. These standards are based on a normal yearly production of 21,000 units of product. The actual level of produciton was 22,000 units, with actual total costs incurred as shown below. Complete the worksheet indicating favorable (F) or unfavorable (U) in column F next to the variance.

	A	B	C	D	E	F
1	Preparer's Name:					
2	Spreadsheet Title: Milton Company, Standard Costs					
3			Standard			
4		Standard	Applied	Actual		
5		Unit $	Costs	Costs	Variances	
6	Direct material	15.00		326,400		
7	Direct labor	35.00		774,000		
8	Variable factory overhead	12.00		262,320		
9	Fixed factory overhead	20.00		409,600		
10	Total					
11	Normal capacity in units	21,000				
12	Actual production in units		22,000			
13					Dollar	
14		Standard	Actual	Variance	Variance	
15	Material Price Variance	5.00	4.80			
16	Material Quantity Variance	66,000	68,000			
17	Labor Rate Variance	17.50	18.00			
18	Labor Efficiency Variance	44,000	43,000			

| Program | the relationships.

Cell Description	Cell	Primary Formulas	Copy To
Total standard unit $	B10	@SUM( )	C10..E10
Direct materials applied	C6	+B6 * $C$12	C7..C9
Direct materials variance	E6		E7..E9
Material Price Variance, Pounds	D15		D16..D18

Material Price Variance, Dollars	E15	
Material Quantity Variance	E16	
Labor Rate Variance	E17	
Labor Efficiency Variance	E18	

Create the electronic worksheet.

☐ Retrieve the template file **VAR.**

☐ First, program the totals in row 10.

☐ Next, program the applied standard costs using the standard unit costs and the actual production units. Standard costs are applied based on the actual number of units produced. Notice that the actual production in units (cell C12) is an absolute reference with dollar signs before the column and the row.

☐ Next, program the variances by comparing the standard costs with the actual costs. If the actual costs are subtracted from the standard costs, a negative variance will indicate an unfavorable variance.

☐ Program the material and labor variances to complete your worksheet.

☐ Save your work. When you are satisfied that your program is correct, save your worksheet by replacing the old file with your newly modified file. Use the same file name and remember to select the **Replace** option.

☐ Complete the analysis sheet.

Solve the problem manually.

At a cash cost of 330,000, Monona, Inc. can acquire equipment that will save $10,000 in annual cash operating expenses. No salvage value is expected at the end of its five-year useful life. Assume the machine will be depreciated over five years on a straight-line basis on both the books and the tax return. Complete the worksheet by writing your answers directly in the boxes.

	A	B	C	D	E	F
1	Preparer's Name:					
2	Spreadsheet Title: Monona, Inc., Capital Budgeting					
3						
4	Annual Income Statement			Investment	330,000	
5	Annual cash savings	100,000		Life in years	5	
6	Depreciation expense			Cutoff interest rate	10.00%	
7	Net income before tax			Income tax rate	30.00%	
8	Income tax expense					
9	Net income after tax			Annual Net Cash Flows		
10	Add back depreciation			Year 1		
11	Annual net cash flow		-------->	Year 2		
12				Year 3		
13	Total present value		<--PV---	Year 4		
14	Less Investment			Year 5		
15	Net present value					
16	Excess present value index					
17						
18	Average rate of return					
19	Cash payback period in yrs					

Program the relationships.

Cell Description	Cell	Primary Formulas
Depreciation expense	B6	
Net income before tax	B7	
Income tax expense	B8	
Net income after tax	B9	
Add back depreciation	B10	
Annual net cash flow	B11	

Cell Description	Cell	Primary Formulas
Total present value	B13	@NPV(E6,E10..E14)
Less Investment	B14	
Net present value	B15	
Excess present value index	B16	
Average rate of return	B18	
Cash payback period	B19	

Create the electronic worksheet.

☐ Retrieve the template file **CAP**.

☐ First, program the income statement for the annual net cash flow.

☐ Next, program the annual net cash flows for the 5 years. First, enter the value from cell B11 for the first year (cell E10). If you make cell B11 an absolute reference, you can then copy this for the remaining four years.

			Copy To
Year 1	E10	+$B$11	E11..E14

Absolute reference

☐ Next, program the total present value of the future cash flows using the following built-in function for present values:
@NPV(E6,E10..E14) where E6 is the interest rate and the range E10..E14 represents the future cash flows. Notice that the interest rate is separated from the cash flows by a comma. The cell address can be typed as shown, or you can include the appropriate cell address by pointing with the arrow keys.

☐ Complete the formulas for the remainder of the worksheet.

☐ Complete the analysis sheet.

Chapter Contents

This chapter consists of nine problem applications for which there are no templates on the *Computer Resource Guide* disk (*CRG* disk). You will create the electronic spreadsheet file using your manual solution as a guide. Page numbers are shown for the problem. There are no analysis sheets for this chapter.

File	Topic	Problem
GPM	Inventory - Gross Profit Method	163
RET	Inventory - Retail Method	164
GDW	Goodwill Calculations	165
POC	Percentage of Contract Completion	166
BVS	Book Value of Stock	167
TND	Trend Percentages	168
RAT	Ratio Analysis	169
JOB	Job Order Costing	170
MLV	Material and Labor Variances	171

Suggested Procedures

You should design your spreadsheet on paper before using the computer. For guidance with your design, use several references. Refer to your textbook for possible formats for the spreadsheet. Use the tutorials in this manual (Chapters 8 and 9) to review skills you may need. Some of the partially programmed template formats on the *CRG* disk may be helpful. Design your model so that it is able to perform instant recalculations with a different set of data inputs.

Design Considerations

Put labels over all columns.
Use the appropriate display format for dollars and percentages.
Widen columns when necessary.
Include an input section, where useful, with the pertinent variable data for calculations.
Define and unprotect those cells that contain data inputs.
Use the copy command to save time.
Dress up your report with underlines and dollar signs where needed.

File: **GPM**   Topic: **Inventory - Gross Profit Method**

| **Create** | the electronic spreadsheet.

Over the past several years, Jordan Company's gross profit has averaged 48% of net sales. During the first six months of the current year, net sales are $750,000, and net cost of purchases totals $400,000. Inventory at the beginning of the period was $60,000. The company prepares quarterly interim financial statements.

| **Required** |

Develop a template, using the gross profit method, to compute the estimated cost of inventory at the end of the current six-month period.

| **What If?** |

The president of Jordan Company would like you to estimate the ending inventory for the following gross profit percentages.

Percent	Ending Inventory
46.50%	$_____.
47.25%	$_____.
48.00%	$_____.
49.25%	$_____.
50.00%	$_____.

Create | the electronic spreadsheet.

Sales clerks for Rochelle Company, a retail concern, took a year-end physical inventory at retail prices and determined that the total retail value of the ending inventory was $120,000. The following information for the year is available:

	Cost	Selling Price
Beginning inventory	$ 73,000	$110,000
Net purchases	421,000	650,000
Sales		631,000

Management estimates its inventory loss from theft and other causes by com-paring its physical ending inventory at retail prices with an estimated ending inventory at retail prices (determined by subtracting sales from goods available for sale at selling prices) and reducing this difference to cost by applying the proper cost ratio.

Required

Develop a template to compute the estimated cost of the ending inventory using the retail method. This inventory amount will appear in the balance sheet, and the calculation should be based on the physical inventory taken at retail prices. In addition, compute the estimated inventory loss for the year from theft and other causes.

What If?

The store manager of Rochelle Company has determined that the year-end physical inventory at retail should have been $123,500. What is the estimated inventory loss now? $_____.

File: **GDW**   Topic: **Goodwill Calculations**

Create the electronic spreadsheet.

Green Company, which is for sale, has identifiable net assets with a fair value of $8,000,000 and no recorded goodwill. Green's annual net income in recent years has averaged $920,000 in an industry that considers 10% a normal rate of return on net assets. In discussing a plan to sell the company, Green argues that goodwill should be recognized by capitalizing the amount of earnings above average at a rate of 15%. On the other hand, the prospective purchaser argues that goodwill should be valued at four times the earnings above average.

Required

Develop a template to compute the earnings above normal, the amount of goodwill claimed by Green Company's owners, and the amount of goodwill according to the purchaser.

What If?

The owners of Green Company would like you to recalculate the estimated goodwill using the following percentages for the average industry earnings on net assets (keep the capitalization rate and multiplier the same):

Industry Average	Goodwill Using A 15% Rate	Goodwill Using A Multiplier of 4
9.25%	$_____	$_____
9.75%	$_____	$_____
10.50%	$_____	$_____
10.75%	$_____	$_____
11.00%	$_____	$_____

File: **POC**   Topic: **Percentage of Contract Completion**

Create the electronic spreadsheet.

On December 1, 19X1, Unicom, Inc., signed a contract to build a communications satellite. Completion and sale of the satellite were scheduled for November 19X3. The total contract price for the satellite was $44,000,000. and total estimated cost was $35,000,000.

The degree of completion is considered equal to the proportion of estimated total cost incurred by the builder. Unicom accounts for operations on a calendar-year basis. Costs for the satellite were incurred and paid as follows:

December 19X1	$ 6,300,000
19X2	18,900,000
19X3	9,800,000

The satellite was finished and the sale was consummated November 8, 19X3.

Required

Develop a template to calculate the gross profit that would be reported each year on accrual basis of accounting using the percentage-of-completion method of revenue recognition.

What If?

The total estimated cost has been revised to $36,100,000 instead of $35,000,000, because the costs incurred for 19X2 were $20,000,000. What is the revised

Gross profit for 19X2.............................$_____.

Gross profit for the total project ....$_____.

File: **BVS**   Topic: **Book Value of Stock**

Create the electronic spreadsheet.

The stockholders' equity section of the Griffin Company contains the following information:

Paid-in Capital:
8% Preferred Stock, $50 Par Value,		
6,000 shares	300,000	
Premium on preferred stock	66,000	366,000
Common Stock, $15 Stated Value,		
25,000 shares	375,000	
Premium on common stock	100,000	475,000
Paid-in Capital from Treasury Stock		19,000
Total Paid-in Capital		860,000
Retained Earnings		130,000
Total Stockholders' Equity		990,000

The preferred stock has a liquidation preference of $52 per share, and dividends are **two** years in arrears.

Required

Develop a template to compute the book value per share for the preferred stock and the common stock. You may find a separate *input* section helpful in designing this template.

What If?

Find the book value per share under the following conditions:

Years in Arrears	Preferred Stock	Common Stock
0	$_____	$_____
1	$_____	$_____
2	$_____	$_____
3	$_____	$_____

| Create | the electronic spreadsheet.

Net sales, net income, and total asset figures for Spectrum Paint, Inc. for five consecutive years are given below:

Annual Amounts (Thousands of Dollars)					
	Year 1	Year 2	Year 3	Year 4	Year 5
Net Sales	52,800	57,300	64,200	69,500	76,800
Net Income	2,430	2,590	3,020	3,350	3,830
Total Assets	32,500	34,200	37,800	40,600	42,400

| Required |

Develop a template to calculate trend percentages, using year 1 as the base year. Also, compute the rate of return on sales for each year.

| What If? |

The owners of Spectrum Paints would like the net sales percentage for Year 6 to be at least 150%. <u>Hint</u>: Change the input in Year 5 until you get the desired percentage.

Net Sales - Year 6 ....\$_____.

Using this new amount for net sales, find the amount of net income necessary for a 5.2% return on sales.

Return on Sales - Year 6 ....\$_____.

File: **RAT**   Topic: **Ratio Analysis**

Create the electronic spreadsheet.

Selected information follows for the Bravo Company, taken from the current year's and last year's financial statements:

	This Year	Last Year
Net Sales	720,000	640,000
Cost of Goods Sold	460,000	416,000
Bond Interest Expense	15,000	15,000
Income Tax Expense	10,000	8,000
Net Income (after income tax)	40,000	32,000
Accounts Receivable, Dec. 31	96,000	82,000
Inventory, Dec. 31	170,000	150,000
Common Stockholders' Equity	340,000	320,000
Total Assets	560,000	480,000

Required

Develop a template to calculate the following ratios and relationships for this year.

1. Return on assets
2. Return on sales
3. Return on common stockholders' equity
4. Average collections period
5. Inventory turnover
6. Bond interest coverage

What If?

Find the projected ratios for next year using the projected amounts below. Hint: **Copy** (don't move) the information for This Year to the column for Last Year, and then enter the new amounts.

Net Sales	810,000
Cost of Goods Sold	500,000
Bond Interest Expense	15,000
Income Tax Expense	12,500
Net Income (after income tax)	50,000
Accounts Receivable, Dec. 31	108,000
Inventory, Dec. 31	185,000
Common Stockholders' Equity	360,000
Total Assets	650,000

RATIOS:
1. Return on assets ...._____%
2. Return on sales ...._____%
3. Return on equity ...._____%
4. Ave. collections period ._____
5. Inventory turnover ...._____
6. Bond interest coverage _____

| **Create** | the electronic spreadsheet.

Butler Manufacturing, Inc. expects the following costs and expenses during the coming year:

Direct Material	45,000
Direct Labor (@ $9/hr.)	153,000
Sales Commissions	34,000
Factory Supervision	22,500
Indirect Labor	42,000
Factory Depreciation	32,000
Factory Taxes	7,500
Factory Insurance	9,000
Factory Supplies Used	8,000
Factory Utilities	15,000

Butler uses a predetermined factory overhead rate applied on the basis of direct labor hours. Job 465 had been charged $12,600 in direct labor.

| **Required** |

Develop a template to compute the predetermined overhead rate based on direct labor hours. Use this rate to calculate the amount of overhead that would be assigned to Job 465.

| **What If?** |

Job 466 had been charged $9,450 in direct labor. What is the amount of

Factory overhead ....$_____

Create the electronic spreadsheet.

Actual and standard cost data for direct material and direct labor relating to the production of 2,000 units of a product are as follows:

	Actual Costs	Standard Costs
Direct material	3,900 pounds @ $5.30	4,000 pounds @ $5
Direct labor	6,200 hours @ $8.40	6,000 hours @ $8.60

Required

Develop a template that will calculate the material price variance, material quantity variance, labor rate variance, and labor efficiency variance.

What If?

The summarized manufacturing data relate to the production of 2,000 finished units of product. Determine the material price and quantity variances, and labor rate and efficiency variances.

Direct material:
      Standard (2 pounds @ $3 per pound)
      Actual (4,200 pounds @ $3.40 per pound)
Direct labor:
      Standard (0.5 hours @ $8 per hour)
      Actual (950 hours @ $7.80 per hour)

Material price variance .... $_____.
Material quantity variance .... $_____.
Labor rate variance .... $_____.
Labor efficiency variance .... $_____.

Part One
FORMS

Categories
Accounts
Transactions

Company Name

Category Definitions

BALANCE SHEET

	BEG#	END#
A - Current Assets		
B - Long-Term Assets		
C - Other Assets		
D - Current Liabilities		
E - Long-Term Liabilities		
F - Owner Equity		

INCOME STATEMENT

	BEG#	END#
G - Operating Revenues		
H - Other Revenues		
I - Operating Costs		
J - Operating Expenses		
k - Other Expenses		

FINANCIAL SUMMARY

DATE: _____

Total Assets		
Total Liabilities		
Owner Equity		

Total Revenues		
Total Expenses		
Net Income		

Chart Of Accounts

ACCT	DESCRIPTION

SYSTEM DESIGNED BY:

Accountant		Date	

Transaction Journal

JOUR				
MOYR				

DAY	ACCT	DESCRIPTION	DEBIT	CREDIT	EXPLANATION

Accountant		Date	

Company Name

Category Definitions

BALANCE SHEET

	BEG#	END#
A – Current Assets		
B – Long-Term Assets		
C – Other Assets		
D – Current Liabilities		
E – Long-Term Liabilities		
F – Owner Equity		

INCOME STATEMENT

	BEG#	END#
G – Operating Revenues		
H – Other Revenues		
I – Operating Costs		
J – Operating Expenses		
k – Other Expenses		

FINANCIAL SUMMARY

DATE: _____

Total Assets		
Total Liabilities		
Owner Equity		

Total Revenues		
Total Expenses		
Net Income		

Chart Of Accounts

ACCT	DESCRIPTION

SYSTEM DESIGNED BY:

Accountant		Date	

Transaction Journal

JOUR [   ]

MOYR [   ]

DAY	ACCT DESCRIPTION	DEBIT	CREDIT	EXPLANATION

Accountant [   ]   Date [   ]

Company Name

Category Definitions

BALANCE SHEET

	BEG#	END#
A – Current Assets		
B – Long-Term Assets		
C – Other Assets		
D – Current Liabilities		
E – Long-Term Liabilities		
F – Owner Equity		

INCOME STATEMENT

	BEG#	END#
G – Operating Revenues		
H – Other Revenues		
I – Operating Costs		
J – Operating Expenses		
k – Other Expenses		

FINANCIAL SUMMARY

DATE: _____

Total Assets		
Total Liabilities		
Owner Equity		

Total Revenues		
Total Expenses		
Net Income		

Chart Of Accounts

ACCT	DESCRIPTION

SYSTEM DESIGNED BY:

Accountant		Date	

Transaction Journal

JOUR [   ]

MOYR [   ]

DAY	ACCT DESCRIPTION	DEBIT	CREDIT	EXPLANATION

Accountant [   ]   Date [   ]

Company Name

Category Definitions

Chart Of Accounts

BALANCE SHEET	BEG#	END#
A – Current Assets		
B – Long-Term Assets		
C – Other Assets		
D – Current Liabilities		
E – Long-Term Liabilities		
F – Owner Equity		

INCOME STATEMENT	BEG#	END#
G – Operating Revenues		
H – Other Revenues		
I – Operating Costs		
J – Operating Expenses		
k – Other Expenses		

ACCT	DESCRIPTION

FINANCIAL SUMMARY

DATE: _____

Total Assets		
Total Liabilities		
Owner Equity		

Total Revenues		
Total Expenses		
Net Income		

SYSTEM DESIGNED BY:

Accountant		Date	

Company Name

Transaction Journal

DAY	ACCT DESCRIPTION	DEBIT	CREDIT	EXPLANATION

Accountant		Date	

182

Company Name

Category Definitions

BALANCE SHEET

	BEG#	END#
A – Current Assets		
B – Long-Term Assets		
C – Other Assets		
D – Current Liabilities		
E – Long-Term Liabilities		
F – Owner Equity		

INCOME STATEMENT

	BEG#	END#
G – Operating Revenues		
H – Other Revenues		
I – Operating Costs		
J – Operating Expenses		
k – Other Expenses		

FINANCIAL SUMMARY

DATE: _____

Total Assets		
Total Liabilities		
Owner Equity		

Total Revenues		
Total Expenses		
Net Income		

Chart Of Accounts

ACCT	DESCRIPTION

SYSTEM DESIGNED BY:

Accountant		Date	

Company Name

Transaction Journal

JOUR [   ]

MOYR [   ]

DAY	ACCT DESCRIPTION	DEBIT	CREDIT	EXPLANATION

Accountant [   ]   Date [   ]

_____
Company Name

Category Definitions

BALANCE SHEET

	BEG#	END#
A – Current Assets		
B – Long-Term Assets		
C – Other Assets		
D – Current Liabilities		
E – Long-Term Liabilities		
F – Owner Equity		

INCOME STATEMENT

	BEG#	END#
G – Operating Revenues		
H – Other Revenues		
I – Operating Costs		
J – Operating Expenses		
k – Other Expenses		

FINANCIAL SUMMARY

DATE: _____

Total Assets		
Total Liabilities		
Owner Equity		

Total Revenues		
Total Expenses		
Net Income		

Chart Of Accounts

ACCT	DESCRIPTION

SYSTEM DESIGNED BY:

Accountant		Date	

Company Name

Transaction Journal

JOUR [　　]

MOYR [　　]

DAY	ACCT DESCRIPTION	DEBIT		CREDIT		EXPLANATION

Accountant [　　　　　　　　　　　　　] Date [　　　　　]

Company Name

Category Definitions

BALANCE SHEET

	BEG#	END#
A – Current Assets		
B – Long-Term Assets		
C – Other Assets		
D – Current Liabilities		
E – Long-Term Liabilities		
F – Owner Equity		

INCOME STATEMENT

	BEG#	END#
G – Operating Revenues		
H – Other Revenues		
I – Operating Costs		
J – Operating Expenses		
k – Other Expenses		

FINANCIAL SUMMARY

DATE: _____

Total Assets		
Total Liabilities		
Owner Equity		

Total Revenues		
Total Expenses		
Net Income		

Chart Of Accounts

ACCT	DESCRIPTION

SYSTEM DESIGNED BY:

Accountant		Date	

Transaction Journal

JOUR [ ]

MOYR [ ]

DAY	ACCT	DESCRIPTION	DEBIT	CREDIT	EXPLANATION

Accountant [   ]   Date [   ]

Company Name

Category Definitions

Chart Of Accounts

ACCT	DESCRIPTION

BALANCE SHEET

BALANCE SHEET	BEG#	END#
A – Current Assets		
B – Long-Term Assets		
C – Other Assets		
D – Current Liabilities		
E – Long-Term Liabilities		
F – Owner Equity		

INCOME STATEMENT

INCOME STATEMENT	BEG#	END#
G – Operating Revenues		
H – Other Revenues		
I – Operating Costs		
J – Operating Expenses		
k – Other Expenses		

FINANCIAL SUMMARY

DATE: _____

Total Assets		
Total Liabilities		
Owner Equity		

Total Revenues		
Total Expenses		
Net Income		

SYSTEM DESIGNED BY:

Accountant		Date	

Transaction Journal

JOUR [ ]
MOYR [ ]

DAY	ACCT	DESCRIPTION	DEBIT	CREDIT	EXPLANATION

Accountant [ ] **Date** [ ]

_____

Company Name

Category Definitions

BALANCE SHEET

	BEG#	END#
A – Current Assets		
B – Long-Term Assets		
C – Other Assets		
D – Current Liabilities		
E – Long-Term Liabilities		
F – Owner Equity		

INCOME STATEMENT

	BEG#	END#
G – Operating Revenues		
H – Other Revenues		
I – Operating Costs		
J – Operating Expenses		
k – Other Expenses		

FINANCIAL SUMMARY

DATE: _____

Total Assets		
Total Liabilities		
Owner Equity		

Total Revenues		
Total Expenses		
Net Income		

Chart Of Accounts

ACCT	DESCRIPTION

SYSTEM DESIGNED BY:

Accountant		Date	

Transaction Journal

JOUR ☐

MOYR ☐

DAY	ACCT DESCRIPTION	DEBIT	CREDIT	EXPLANATION

Accountant ☐ Date ☐

Category Definitions

Chart Of Accounts

BALANCE SHEET	BEG#	END#
A – Current Assets		
B – Long-Term Assets		
C – Other Assets		
D – Current Liabilities		
E – Long-Term Liabilities		
F – Owner Equity		

INCOME STATEMENT	BEG#	END#
G – Operating Revenues		
H – Other Revenues		
I – Operating Costs		
J – Operating Expenses		
k – Other Expenses		

ACCT	DESCRIPTION

FINANCIAL SUMMARY

DATE: _____

Total Assets		
Total Liabilities		
Owner Equity		

Total Revenues		
Total Expenses		
Net Income		

SYSTEM DESIGNED BY:

Accountant		Date	

Transaction Journal

Company Name

JOUR			
MOYR			

DAY	ACCT	DESCRIPTION	DEBIT	CREDIT	EXPLANATION

Accountant		Date	

Company Name
_____

Category Definitions

BALANCE SHEET

	BEG#	END#
A – Current Assets		
B – Long-Term Assets		
C – Other Assets		
D – Current Liabilities		
E – Long-Term Liabilities		
F – Owner Equity		

INCOME STATEMENT

	BEG#	END#
G – Operating Revenues		
H – Other Revenues		
I – Operating Costs		
J – Operating Expenses		
k – Other Expenses		

FINANCIAL SUMMARY

DATE: _____

Total Assets		
Total Liabilities		
Owner Equity		

Total Revenues		
Total Expenses		
Net Income		

Chart Of Accounts

ACCT	DESCRIPTION

SYSTEM DESIGNED BY:

Accountant		Date	

Transaction Journal

JOUR [ ]

MOYR [ ]

DAY	ACCT DESCRIPTION	DEBIT	CREDIT	EXPLANATION

Accountant [ ]   Date [ ]

Company Name

Category Definitions

BALANCE SHEET

BALANCE SHEET	BEG#	END#
A – Current Assets		
B – Long-Term Assets		
C – Other Assets		
D – Current Liabilities		
E – Long-Term Liabilities		
F – Owner Equity		

INCOME STATEMENT	BEG#	END#
G – Operating Revenues		
H – Other Revenues		
I – Operating Costs		
J – Operating Expenses		
k – Other Expenses		

FINANCIAL SUMMARY

DATE: _____

Total Assets		
Total Liabilities		
Owner Equity		

Total Revenues		
Total Expenses		
Net Income		

Chart Of Accounts

ACCT	DESCRIPTION

SYSTEM DESIGNED BY:

Accountant		Date	

Transaction Journal

JOUR [   ]

MOYR [   ]

DAY	ACCT DESCRIPTION	DEBIT	CREDIT	EXPLANATION

Accountant		Date	

Part Two
FORMS

**Electronic
Spreadsheet
Analysis**

Name:_____ Class:_____ Date:_____

File: **BAN**   Title: **Bank Reconciliation**

| your solutions.

VERIFY YOUR WORK. Compare your electronic and manual solutions.

(1) What is the amount for the adjusted bank balance and for the adjusted book balance?
$_____.

(2) What is the unreconciled difference? $_____.

PERFORM "WHAT-IF" ANALYSIS. Now that you have verified your program and have an understanding of the relationships, try entering these changes into your spreadsheet and let the computer calculate the results.

(3) If the balance per the bank statement had been $6,138.24, how much would the unreconciled difference be? $_____.

(4) Keeping the bank statement balance of $6,138.24, change the other information as follows:

Outstanding checks	$1,093.60
Deposits in transit	$2,170.00

Sullivan discovered a deposit of $426 made on July 31 that the bank had recorded but that Sullivan had forgot to record on the books.

What is the total adjusted bank balance now? $_____.

What is the unreconciled difference now? $_____.

(5) Work the alternative problem on the back.

Prepare the worksheet for data entry.

Generally, the input values will be displayed in higher intensity (brighter than normal) on the worksheet. Before working the alternative problem, erase the cell contents for the input values from the last problem. This is easy to do. Move to the first cell to be erased, cell B5. Then select **/ R E** (Range Erase command) and press the **<Down>** arrow key to highlight those input cells that you would like to erase. Press the **<Return>** key and the cell contents will be erased. Repeating this procedure for each range of inputs will provide you with a programmed worksheet ready for data entry.

Alternative Problem - Bank Reconciliation

On May 31, the Cash in Bank account of Wallace Company, a sole proprietorship, had a balance of $6,122.50. On that date, the bank statement indicated a balance of $8,180.40. Comparison of returned checks and bank advices revealed the following:

(1) Deposits in transit May 31 amounted to $2,585.60.
(2) Outstanding checks May 31 totaled $3,211.70.
(3) The bank added to the account $27.80 of interest income earned by Wallace during May.
(4) The bank collected a $2,400 note receivable for Wallace and charged a $20 collection fee. Both items appear on the bank statement.
(5) Bank service charges in addition to the collection fee, not yet recorded on the books, were $20.
(6) Included with the returned checks is a memo indicating that L. Ryder's check for $686 had been returned NSF. Ryder, a customer, had sent the check to pay an account of $700 less a 2% discount.
(7) Wallace Company recorded the payment of an account payable as $690; the check was for $960.

Prepare a bank reconciliation for Wallace Company at May 31.

What is the amount for the adjusted bank balance? $_____.

Name:_____ Class:_____ Date:_____

File: **REC**   Title: **Accounts Receivable Credit Losses**

Analyze your solutions.

VERIFY YOUR WORK. Compare your electronic and manual solutions.
(1) What is the total expected loss on accounts receivable? $_____.
(2) What is the net amount of accounts receivable over six months? $_____.

PREDICT RESULTS. Without using the computer, answer these questions.

(3) If the expected loss percentage for the current accounts receivable were changed to 2%, the
    expense provision would _____(increase/decrease).
(4) What would the net amount of the 0-60 days past due accounts be if that loss is expected to be
    10% instead of the 5%? $_____.

PERFORM "WHAT-IF" ANALYSIS. Enter these changes.

(5) If the balance in the Allowance for Uncollectible Accounts is a debit balance of $1,500, what is
    the expense provision? $_____.

(6) Work the alternative problem on the back.

Alternative Problem - Accounts Receivable Credit Losses

At December 31,1993 Rinehart Company had a balance of $304,000 in its Accounts Receivable account and a credit balance of $2,800 in the Allowance for Uncollectible Accounts. The accounts receivable subsidiary ledger consisted of $309,600 in debit balances and $5,600 in credit balances. The company has aged its accounts as follows:

Current	$272,000
0-60 days past due	18,000
61-180 days past due	11,200
Over six months past due	8,400

In the past, the company has experienced losses as follows: 2% of current balances, 6% of balances 0-60 days past due, 15% of balances 61-180 days past due, and 30% of balances more than six months past due. The company bases its provision for credit losses on the aging analysis.

What is the total expected loss from uncollectible accounts?
$_____.

What is the expense provision for uncollectible accounts?
$_____.

Name:_____ Class:_____ Date:_____

File: **LCM**   Title: **Inventory - Lower of Cost or Market**

| **Analyze** | your solutions.

VERIFY YOUR WORK. Compare your electronic and manual solutions.

(1) What is the grand total of the total cost? $_____.

(2) What is the lower of cost or market for

    Each item? $_____.

    Each category? $_____.

    Grand total? $_____.

PREDICT RESULTS. Without using the computer, answer these questions.

(3) If the quantity increased for any of the fans or heaters, would you expect that both total cost and total market would change? _____ (yes/no)

(4) If the unit market price on Model X2 fans increased to $23, which total inventory valuation would be lower for fans? _____ (cost or market)

PERFORM "WHAT-IF" ANALYSIS. Try entering these changes.

(5) Suppose the quantities for the three models of the fans were as follows:

    Model X1: 350 units, Model X2: 325 units, Model X3: 300 units.

    What is the total cost for the fans? $_____.

    What is the total market for the fans? $_____.

(6) Change the following information:

    Unit cost on Model B7 heaters is $23, unit market on Model B8 heaters is $31, unit cost on Model B9 heaters is $43, and the unit market on Model B9 is $44.

    What is the total cost for Model B7? $_____.

    What is the total market for Model B8? $_____.

    What is the lower of cost or market for Model B9? $_____.

(7) Work the alternative problem on the back.

Alternative Problem - Inventory, Lower of Cost or Market

Crane Company had the following inventory at December 31, 1993:

		Unit Price	
Desks	Quantity	Cost	Market
Model 9001	70	$190	$200
Model 9002	45	280	268
Model 9003	20	350	360
Cabinets			
Model 7001	120	60	64
Model 7002	80	95	88
Model 7003	50	130	126

What is the ending inventory by applying the lower of cost or market rule to:

(1)   Each item of inventory? $_____.

(2)   Each major category of inventory? $_____.

(3)   The total inventory? $_____.

Which of the LCM methods results in the lowest net income for 1993? Explain.

Name:_____ Class:_____ Date:_____

File: **DEP**   Title: **Depreciation**

┌─────────┐
│ **Analyze** │ your solutions.
└─────────┘

VERIFY YOUR WORK. Compare your electronic and manual solutions.

(1) What is the straight-line book value at the end of Year 4? $_____.

(2) What is the total double declining depreciaton expense for the four years? $_____.

PREDICT RESULTS. Without using the computer, answer these questions.

(3) If the estimated life is eight years, what will the double declining depreciation rate be?
      _____%

(4) With a salvage value of $6,400, what would the straight-line book value be at the end of the
      estimated life of eight years? $_____.

PERFORM "WHAT-IF" ANALYSIS. Enter these changes.

(5) With a cost of $80,000 and a salvage value of $5,000, what is the total depreciation expense
      for

	Straight Line	Double Declining
3-year life	_____	_____
4-year life	_____	_____
5-year life	_____	_____

(6)   Work the alternative problem on the back.

Alternative Problem - Depreciation

On January 2, 1993, Alvarez Company purchased an electroplating machine to help manufacture a part for one of its key products. The machine cost $109,350 and was estimated to have a useful life of six years, after which it could be sold for $11,700. Calculate the first three years of depreciation expense for straight-line and double-declining-balance methods of depreciation.

Year	Straight Line	Double Declining
1	_____	_____
2	_____	_____
3	_____	_____

Will changing the salvage value have an effect on the straight-line depreciation expense? _____(yes/no). Why?

Will changing the salvage value have an effect on the double declining depreciation expense? _____(yes/no). Why?

Name:_____ Class:_____ Date:_____

File: **PAY**   Title: **Payroll Accounting**

Analyze your solutions.

VERIFY YOUR WORK. Compare your electronic and manual solutions.

(1) What are the total gross earnings? $_____.
(2) What are the total net earnings? $_____.

PREDICT RESULTS. Without using the computer, answer these questions.

(3) If John Scott has worked 2 hours of overtime, what would you expect his overtime earnings to be? _____.

(4) If Ann Poole had not worked any overtime, what would you expect her gross earnings to be? _____.

PERFORM "WHAT-IF" ANALYSIS. Try entering these changes into your spreadsheet and let the computer calculate the results.

(5) The timekeeper for Edgewater Company has given you the following information to use for the payroll for the week ended March 31:

	Hours Worked	New Hourly Rate
James Allen	40	
Paul Durango	42	$8.00
Ann Poole	45	
John Scott	41	
Amy Thorp	40	$6.75

Assuming that any hours over 40 are overtime and that the federal income tax and medical deductions remain the same, determine the total cash needed to meet the net payroll (net earnings). $_____.

(6) Work the alternative problem on the back.

209

Alternative Problem - Payroll Accounting

Herman Company employs five persons, all of whom are paid an hourly rate. All employees receive overtime pay at one and a half times their regular pay rate. Data relating to the payroll for the week ended March 31 are given below:

Employee	Hours Worked	Pay Rate
Janice Carter	43	$10.00 per hour
Dale Farmer	40	$12.00 per hour
George Monroe	40	$ 8.00 per hour
James Rider	42	$ 8.00 per hour
Robert Warren	40	$10.00 per hour

All salaries and wages are subject to FICA tax; a 7.65% rate is assumed. Each employee has a $4.00 per week deduction for group medical insurance. Assume the federal income tax withheld the last week in March is:

Carterr	$ 52.00
Farmer	60.00
Monroe	39.00
Rider	37.00
Warren	37.00

Process the payroll for the last week in March.

What is the total gross earnings for the period? $_____.

What is the total net payroll for the period? $_____.

Name:_____ Class:_____ Date:_____

File: **INS**   Title: **Installment Sales**

[**Analyze**] **your solutions.**

VERIFY YOUR WORK. Compare your electronic and manual solutions.

(1) What is the total gross profit percentage? _____%

(2) What is the cost of property sold for 1995? $_____.

PREDICT RESULTS. Without using the computer, answer these questions.

(3) If the down payment had been 35%, would you expect that the amount of gross profit in 1994 would (increase/decrease)? _____.

PERFORM "WHAT-IF" ANALYSIS. Try entering these changes.

(4) For tax planning purposes, your supervisor requests you to prepare an analysis on the basis that only 10% is paid on the date of sale, that $15, 000 is collected in 1994, and that the balance is collected in 1995. What is the gross profit for:

1993 $_____.

1994 $_____.

1995 $_____.

(5) Using the changes in Question 4, your supervisor now requests you to modify your analysis by changing the total cost of property sold to $193,000. What would the gross profit be for:

1993 $_____.

1994 $_____.

1995 $_____.

Name:_____ Class:_____ Date:_____

File: **PAR**   Title: **Partnership Income Allocation**

┌─────────┐
│ **Analyze** │ **your solutions.**
└─────────┘

VERIFY YOUR WORK. Compare your electronic and manual solutions.

(1) What is the total ending capital balance? $_____.

(2) What is net income (loss) for Thomas? $_____.

PERFORM "WHAT-IF" ANALYSIS. Try entering these changes into your spreadsheet and let the computer calculate the results.

(3) Just before sending your capital schedule to the partners, you discovered an error in the net income calculation. The correct net income is $28,000. What are the corrected net income allocations ?

Dole $_____.   Fine $_____.   Thomas $_____.

(4) Because of the error in the net income, you have carefully reviewed all of the paperwork for the partnership and found that the partners have renegotiated the profit and loss ratios during the year. Dole now has 60%, Fine 25%, and Thomas 15%. What is the net income allocation and ending capital balance for each partner now that you have corrected the net income and the profit and loss ratios?

	Net Income	Ending Capital
Dole	$_____.	$_____.
Fine	$_____.	$_____.
Thomas	$_____.	$_____.

(5) Work the alternative problem on the back.

Alternative Problem - Partnership Income Allocation

The capital accounts and the Income Summary account as of December 31, 1993, of the Baker, Kane, and Quinn partnership appear below. None of the partners withdrew capital during 1993. The net income for the year is $72,000.

	January 1 Balance	Contributions
Baker	120,000	120,000
Kane	60,000	40,000
Quinn	48,000	0

If there are no allowances and the net income is shared equally, how is the net income allocated?

Baker $_____   Kane $_____   Quinn $_____

If there are no allowances and the net income is shared in the ratio 3:2:1, respectively, how is the net income allocated?

Baker $_____   Kane $_____   Quinn $_____

If an agreement allows $36,000 salary to Baker, 10% interest on beginning investments, with the remainder shared equally, how is the net income allocated?

Baker $_____   Kane $_____   Quinn $_____

What are the ending capital balances?

Baker $_____   Kane $_____   Quinn $_____

Name:_____ Class:_____ Date:_____

File: **EPS**   Title: **Earnings per Share**

| Analyze | your solutions.

VERIFY YOUR WORK. Compare your electronic and manual solutions.

(1) What is the earnings per share of common stock for the net income? $_____.

(2) What is the gross profit on sales? $_____.

PREDICT RESULTS. Without using the computer, answer this question.

(3) If the 4,000 shares of common stock shown to be issued in May were actually issued in February, what effect would this error have on the reported earnings per share? The reported earnings are too_____(low/high).

PERFORM "WHAT-IF" ANALYSIS. Try entering these changes.

(4) The stock transfer agent has verified that the shares in Question 3 were actually issued in February, not in May as shown. Make this correction to your worksheet. Now what are the earnings per share for net income? $_____.

(5) The investors of Bowden Company would like you to calculate the earnings per share for net income if the extraordinary loss has been only $30,000. $_____.

(6) Your supervisor has reviewed your work and is very interested in seeing "what-if" the company had produced the following results:

Sales	$ 810,000	Administrative expenses	$72,000
Cost of goods sold	485,000	Loss on sale of equipment	5,000
Selling expenses	58,000	Extraordinary loss item	37,000

You are asked to provide the following earnings per share information:

Income before extraordinary $_____.

Extraordinary loss $_____.

Net income $_____.

(7) Work the alternative problem on the back.

Alternative Problem - Earnings per Share

Garner Corporation discloses earnings per share amounts for extra-ordinary items. The following summarized data are related to the company's 1993 operations:

Sales	$ 1,480,000
Cost of goods sold	860,000
Selling expenses	120,000
Administrative expenses	95,000
Gain from expropriation of property by foreign government (considered unusual and infrequent)	125,000
Loss from plant strike	65,000

Shares of common stock:

Outstanding at January 1, 1993	46,000 shares
Additional issued at April 1, 1993	17,000 shares
Additional issued at August 1, 1993	3,000 shares

Prepare a multiple-step income statement for Garner Corporation for 1993. Assume a 40% income tax rate. Include earnings per share disclosures for 1993 at the bottom of the income statement.

You are asked to provide the following information:

Net income	$_____.
Average common shares	$_____.
Earnings per share	$_____.

Name:_____ Class:_____ Date:_____

File: **BON**   Title: **Bonds Payable**

[**Analyze**] **your solutions.**

VERIFY YOUR WORK. Using the data inputs given in the problem, compare your electronic and manual solutions.

(1) What is the interest expense for Year 1 Period 1? $_____.

(2) What is book value at the end of Year 2 Period 4? $_____.

PREDICT RESULTS. Without using the computer, answer these questions.

(3) If the bond contract interest rate is increased from 8% to 8.5%, the bond sales price would _____ (increase/decrease).

(4) If the bond contract interest rate is increased from 8% to 10.5%, the bonds would sell at a _____ (premium/discount).

PERFORM "WHAT-IF" ANALYSIS. Try entering these changes into your spreadsheet and let the computer calculate the results.

(5) Using the inputs given in the problem, split the window so that the inputs and the bottom of the amortization schedule are both visible. Change the selling price so that the discount is almost fully amortized. (Experiment by changing the selling price to see how sensitive the discount is to the changes.) What is the selling price at the point where the discount is almost fully amortized? $_____.

(6) Work the alternative problem on the back.

Alternative Problem - Bonds Payable

On December 31, 1993. Echo, Inc. issued $700,000 face value, 11%, 10-year bonds for $659,995, yielding an effective interest rate of 12%. Semi-annual interest is payable on June 30 and December 31 each year. The firm uses the effective interest method to amortize the discount. Prepare an amortization schedule.

What is the interest expense for Year 2 Period 4? $_____.

What is the book value at the end of Year 2? $_____.

Assume that the bonds were issued for $743,618, yielding an effective interest rate of 10%.

What is the interest expense for Year 2 Period 4? $_____.

What is the book value at the end of Year 2? $_____.

Name:_____ Class:_____ Date:_____

File: **CBS**   Title: **Consolidated Balance Sheet**

Analyze your solutions.

VERIFY YOUR WORK. Compare your electronic and manual solutions.

(1) What is the amount of total consolidated assets? $_____.

(2) What is the amount of goodwill from consolidation? $_____.

(3) What is the amount of the minority interest? $_____.

PREDICT RESULTS. Without using the computer, answer these questions.

(4) If Katt Company had paid $510,000 for the purchase of the stock, would there still be an entry for Goodwill?_____ (yes/no)?

(5) If Katt Company had purchased 80% of the common stock of Harbor Company for $490,000, you would expect the minority interest to _____ (increase/decrease) by _____%.

PERFORM "WHAT-IF" ANALYSIS. Try entering these changes.

(6) Suppose Katt Company actually paid $520,000 for 75% of the common stock of Harbor Company. Make the necessary changes to your worksheet and answer the following:

Investment in Harbor $_____.

Goodwill $_____.

Minority interest $_____.

(7) Work the alternative problem on the back.

Alternative Problem - Consolidated Balance Sheet

On January 1, 1994, Weaver, Inc. purchased 75% of the voting stock of Ogden, Inc. for $530,000, after which the separate balance sheets of the two companies were as follows:

	Weaver	Ogden
Accounts Receivable	$ 90,000	$ 40,000
Investment in Ogden, Inc.	530,000	
Other Assets	995,000	760,000
	$1,615,000	$800,000
Accounts Payable	240,000	$ 140,000
Common Stock	900,000	600,000
Retained Earnings	475,000	60,000
	$1,615,000	$800,000

At January 1, 1994, Ogden, Inc. owed $10,000 to Weaver, Inc. on account for purchases made during 1993. Prepare a consolidated balance sheet worksheet at January 1, 1994. Assume that any amount paid by Weaver in excess of the equity acquired in Ogden is attributable to goodwill.

Complete the following:

Consolidated goodwill $_____.

Minority interest $_____.

Consolidated assets $_____.

Name:_____ Class:_____ Date:_____

File: **MFG**   Title: **Manufacturing Costs**

[**Analyze**] your solutions.

VERIFY YOUR WORK. Compare your electronic and manual solutions.
(1) What is the total cost per unit for finished goods? $_____.
(2) What is the total cost for work in progress? $_____.

PREDICT RESULTS. Without using the computer, answer these questions.

(3) If the total finished units is 8,000 units rather than 7,000 units, what would the total cost for finished goods be? $_____.
(4) If the factory overhead rate is increased to 90%, what would the unit total cost be for:
Work in progress? $_____. Finished goods? $_____.

PERFORM "WHAT-IF" ANALYSIS. Enter these changes.

(5) Confirm your answers for questions 3 and 4 and then change the units back to 7,000.

(6)   The general manager believes that the predetermined factory overhead rate is incorrect and has asked you to prepare an analysis of total inventory costs based on the rates shown below. Complete the schedule.

Factory OH Rate	Work In Progress	Finished Goods
87.50%		
85.00%		
80.00%		
77.50%		
75.00%		

Name:_____ Class:_____ Date:_____

File: **PRO**   Title: **Process Cost Accounting**

[**Analyze**] **your solutions.**

VERIFY YOUR WORK. Compare your electronic and manual solutions.

(1) What is the total cost of goods transferred out? $_____.

(2) What is the ending inventory cost? $_____.

PREDICT RESULTS. Without using the computer, complete these questions.

(3) If the ending inventory was 35% complete, the dollar amount transferred out would

_____ (increase/decrease). The equivalent unit cost of conversion would

_____ (increase/decrease).

PERFORM "WHAT-IF" ANALYSIS. Enter these changes.

(4) Confirm your answers in Question 3 by making the change.

(5) The production manager believes that the 30% completion for ending inventory is too low and
would like you to prepare an analysis using different percentages. Complete the table.

Percent Complete	Ending Inventory	Cost of Goods Transferred Out
32%	_____	_____
34%	_____	_____
36%	_____	_____
38%	_____	_____

(6) Complete the alternative problem on the back.

Alternative Problem - Process Cost Accounting

Bradford Company processed a scouring powder through its Compounding Department and Packaging Department. In the Packaging Department, costs of direct materials, direct labor, and factory overhead are incurred evenly throughout the process. Bradford uses the FIFO method. Costs charged to the Packaging Department in October were:

Inventory, October 1	
(5,000 units, 25% complete)	$ 4,250
Transferred in (82,000 units)	164,000
Direct material	81,550
Direct labor	31,770
Factory overhead	33,470

	$ 315,040
	========

At October 31, 7,000 units were in process, 40% completed.

Notes:

(1)   The beginning inventory was 75% completed during this period.

(2)   Because the direct material cost was incurred evenly, it can be combined with labor and overhead costs in determing the cost input for conversion.

(3)   The cost transferred in of $164,000 can be treated as a material cost input. This cost is directly related to the 82,000 units transferred in.

What are the equivalent units converted during October? _____.

What is the cost of units transferred out? $_____.

What is the cost of the ending inventory? $_____.

Name:_____ Class:_____ Date:_____

File: **CVP**   Title: **Cost-Volume-Profit Relationships**

┌─────────────┐
│ **Analyze** │ your solutions.
└─────────────┘

VERIFY YOUR WORK. Compare your electronic and manual solutions.

(1) What is the contribution margin rate? _____%

(2) What is the break-even sales in dollars? $_____.

PREDICT RESULTS. Without using the computer, answer these questions.

(3) Will changing actual total unit sales affect the break-even amounts? _____(yes/no)

(4) Will changing the total fixed costs affect the contribution ratio? _____(yes/no)

PERFORM "WHAT-IF" ANALYSIS. Enter these changes.

(5) Change the total fixed costs to $40,000. How much is the net income at 200% (double) the
break-even sales level? $_____. At the 0% sales level? $_____.
Now change the fixed costs to $8,000. Explain why the net income at double the break-even
sales level and at the zero sales level is always the same as the total fixed costs.

(6) With fixed costs of $72,000, change the total unit sales to 2,000 units. How much is the net
income? $_____. About how many units would we have to sell to have net income of
about $19,800? _____units. (Experiment by changing the total unit sales to see how
sensitive the net income is to the units sold.)

(7) Work the alternative problem on the back.

Alternative Problem - Cost-Volume-Profit Relationships

Midvale Corporation sells a single product for $100 per unit, of which $40 is contribution margin. Total fixed costs are $120,000 and net income before tax is $48,000. Before using your worksheet, you will need to calculate the unit variable cost and the number of units sold at the present sales level.

What is the present sales volume in dollars? $_____.

What is the break-even point in units? _____units.

What is the break-even point in dollars? $_____.

What is the approximate sales volume necessary to attain a net income before taxes of $60,000? _____units. $_____.

Name:_____ Class:_____ Date:_____

File: **AVC**   Title: **Absorption/Variable Costing**

[**Analyze**] your solutions.

VERIFY YOUR WORK. Compare your electronic and manual solutions.

Answer the following questions for Year 1992

(1) What is the gross profit for:
Absorption costing? $_____.
Variable costing? $_____.
Difference? $_____.

(2) Production exceeded sales in 1992 by? _____units.

(3) Fixed cost per unit for 1992 is? $_____.
The answer to Question 2 times the answer to Question 3 should be the difference in Question 1.

PREDICT RESULTS. Without using the computer, answer these questions.

(4) If the 1993 sales are 110,000 units, which costing method will have the largest gross profit?_____ (absorption/variable), and by how much? $_____.

PERFORM "WHAT-IF" ANALYSIS. Enter these changes.

(5) Confirm your answers in Question 4 by entering the change in units sold for 1993.

(6) Leaving the change of 110,000 units sold for 1993, enter the following corrections for 1993:
Unit manufacturing cost $52.50
Unit variable manufacturing cost   33.30
Unit sales price   81.00
What is the gross profit for 1993:
Absorption costing $_____.
Variable costing $_____.

(7) Work the alternative problem on the back.

Alternative Problem - Absorption/Variable Costing

Frances Manufacturing makes a product with total unit manufacturing costs of $64, of which $36 is variable. No units were on hand at the beginning of 1992. During 1992 and 1993, the only product manufactured was sold for $96 per unit, and the cost structure did not change. The company uses the first-in, first-out inventory method and has the following production and sales for 1992 and 1993:

	Units Manufactured	Units Sold
1992	100,000	70,000
1993	100,000	120,000

What is the gross profit for:

	1992	1993
Absorption costing	$_____	$_____
Variable costing	$_____	$_____
Difference	$_____	$_____

Name:_____ Class:_____ Date:_____

File: **VAR**   Title: **Standard Costs and Variances**

Analyze your solutions.

VERIFY YOUR WORK. Compare your electronic and manual solutions.

(1) What is the total overall variance? $_____.
    Is it favorable or unfavorable? _____.

(2) What is total standard applied costs? $_____.

(3) What is the material quantity variance? $_____.

PREDICT RESULTS. Without using the computer, answer these questions.

(4) Will increasing the standard unit cost for direct material change the overall variance?
    _____(yes/no) _____(increase/decrease)

PERFORM "WHAT-IF" ANALYSIS. Enter these changes.

(5) Your review of the actual costs for direct materials indicates that the figures shown are
    incorrect. The correct numbers for materials show 70,660 pounds at $5.05 per pound for a
    total actual cost of $356,833. What are the correct numbers for:

Total variance	$_____.
Total material variance	$_____.
Material price variance	$_____.
Material quantity variance	$_____.

(6)   Work the alternative problem on the back.

Alternative Problem - Standard Costs and Variances

Sanchez Company planned to produce 10,000 units of its only product during the year. Sanchez established the following standard cost data for this product prior to the beginning of the year:

	Per Unit
Direct material (2 pounds at $7.50 per pound)	$15.00
Direct labor (1.5 hours at $13.50 per hour)	20.25
Variable overhead (1.5 hours at $6 per hour)	9.00
Fixed overhead (1.5 hours at $9 per hour)	13.50
Total standard cost per unit	$57.75

The actual level of production was 9,000 units, with the following actual total costs incurred:

	Total Cost
Direct material (17,000 pounds at $7.80)	$132,600
Direct labor (14,000 hours at $13.35)	186,900
Variable overhead	80,250
Fixed overhead	145,650
Total actual cost	$ 545,400

The expected level of operations was 15,000 direct labor hours and the normal (multiyear average) level of operations was 16,000 direct labor hours.

What is the total overall variance? $_____(favorable/unfavorable).

What is the total standard applied costs? $_____.

What is the labor efficiency variance? $_____.

Name:_____ Class:_____ Date:_____

File: **CAP**   Title: **Capital Budgeting**

Analyze your solutions.

VERIFY YOUR WORK. Compare your electronic and manual solutions.

(1) What is the annual net cash flow? $_____.

(2) What is the excess present value index? _____.

(3) What is the cash payback period in years? _____.

PREDICT RESULTS. Without using the computer, answer these questions.

(4) Will increasing the cutoff interest rate change the total present value? _____(yes/no)
    If yes, it will _____ (increase/decrease).

(5) Will decreasing the income tax rate change the net present value? _____(yes/no)
    If yes, it will _____ (increase/decrease).

PERFORM "WHAT-IF" ANALYSIS. Enter these changes.

(6) Confirm your answers in question 4 and 5 by making the changes.

(7) Your department manager believes that the investment will not be approved with the excess present value index shown in your original analysis with a cutoff interest rate of 10% and an income tax rate of 30%. He also believes that the annual cash savings of $100,000 is too low. He would like you to determine the approximate annual cash savings required to produce an excess present value index of **1.16**. $_____. (Experiment by changing the input for cash savings.)

The Computer Environment

Ten years ago the word *microcomputer* was not listed in the dictionary. Today, students of all ages are exposed to and use microcomputers. A microcomputer is really nothing more than a machine made up of mechanical and electrical parts, designed to bring a certain amount of convenience and efficiency to our business and personal lives. Some choose to ignore the world of computing while others, realizing that they cannot escape, accept the computer and use the intended benefits to the fullest extent possible. The power of the microcomputer lies in the endless variety of computing applications. In fact, the microcomputer has invaded every aspect of our lives.

Basically, there are three parts to a microcomputer system: hardware, software, and you (the user of the system).

Hardware   Software

The User

Understanding each hardware and software component will give you, the user, a better working knowledge and appreciation of the computer environment as a whole.

Hardware

The Four Basic Components

Generally, the IBM PC microcomputer system consists of four visible and distinct components as shown below. You will use the **keyboard** to communicate with the computer by typing instructions and requests for information. The computer will then use the **monitor** and the **printer** to communicate with you by either displaying or printing your requests. The **system unit** processes all of your instructions and coordinates both the inputs and the outputs.

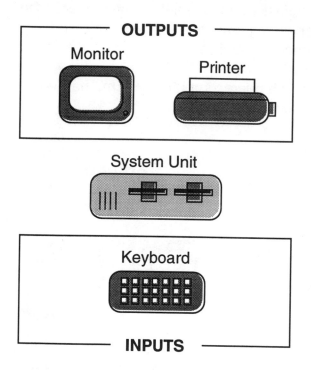

The **monitor** and **printer** are used by the computer to communicate its response to your instructions and requests.

The **system unit** contains the central processing unit as well as the computer memory and disk drives.

The **keyboard** is used to communicate your instructions and requests to the computer.

Using the keyboard, you control the processing sequence by sending your requests to the computer. The IBM PC keyboard contains some unusual keys. Let's look at some of the keys you will be using.

The Keyboard

In addition to the standard typewriter keys (not shown below), the keyboard contains special keys that may need some explanation. The diagram below shows the location of some of the unusual keys found on the standard IBM PC keyboard.

IBM PC Keyboard Layout

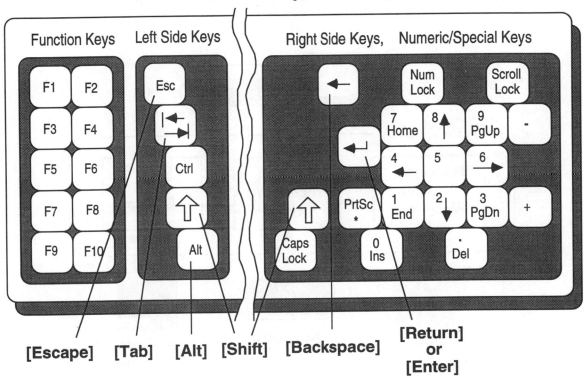

The function keys (found on the left side) have specific functions depending on the software program. In Chapter 2, Lesson 3, the keyboard is more fully described, with an explanation of the different keys grouped by major function.

There are many models of the IBM microcomputer. The keyboard shown above is the standard keyboard for the IBM PC. Other models such as the IBM XT or IBM AT may use an extended keyboard with some of the keys located differently than shown above. For example, on the extended keyboard, the function keys are located across the top and the 10-key numeric keypad is separate from the pointer movement keys.

The System Unit

      The system unit contains three distinct parts: The central processing unit (**CPU**), random access memory (**RAM**), and the **disk drives**. The **CPU** processes your instructions and directs the interaction of all of the system components. The **RAM** is a temporary storage area used by the **CPU** in processing data. The disk drives allow data to be read into the computer and data to be written back to the floppy disk as a permanent record.

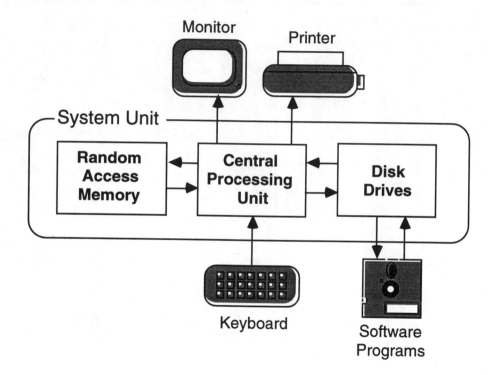

      Your instructions are sent from the keyboard to the **CPU**. The **CPU** then processes your instructions using the **RAM** to temporarily store the instructions as well as the results. For example, your instructions may require the **CPU** to read information from a floppy disk that has been inserted into a disk drive. In this case the **CPU** would read the information from the floppy disk into the **RAM** to facilitate processing.

      The **RAM** is often referred to as <u>main memory</u>, which is temporary, while the disk storage is considered to be permanent. Understanding this difference is crucial.

Random Access Memory and Floppy Disk Storage

The "current" work that is displayed on the monitor exists in the computer's RAM, or main memory. If you turn off your computer or have a power failure before saving your work, it will be lost. You must first save your work to a floppy disk for a permanent record. Think of the floppy disk as a storage cabinet and each file as a separate folder in the storage cabinet. Each time you retrieve a file from the floppy disk, an exact copy is transferred to the RAM memory to be processed. The original stays safely on the disk, where it can be retrieved again, or replaced with your updated work.

Disk Drives

A disk drive can either **read** data from or **write** data to a magnetic disk. Notice that the arrows (data flow) are shown going both ways in the diagram on the preceding page. There are two types of disk drives: floppy disk drives and hard disk drives. Floppy disk drives allow you to transfer software programs and data files from a floppy disk to the CPU for processing. A hard disk drive reads and writes data to a large magnetic disk, which is permanently mounted inside the disk drive.

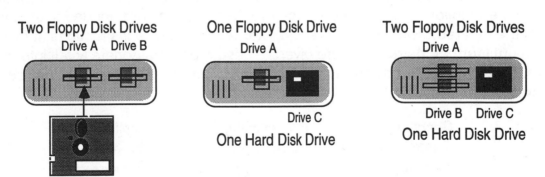

Each disk drive has a name such as **A**, **B**, or **C**. The drive name is used to instruct the CPU where to read or write data. There are generally three different disk drive arrangements. You may have two floppy disk drives, **Drive A** and **Drive B**. Some systems have a single floppy drive with a hard disk drive inside of the system unit. Hard disk drives usually are called **Drive C**. Another arrangement could be two floppy disk drives and a hard disk drive. In this case, the floppy disk drives are usually mounted top and bottom as shown above.

Handling Floppy Disks

Use reasonable care in handling your floppy disks because they can be easily damaged. Heat, dust, or fingerprints can destroy the data making the disk unusable. Use the "rule of thumb" method of loading the disk into the disk drive. Gently open the disk drive door and insert the exposed oval area of the disk while holding the thumb over the label. When you are finished, remove the disk and put it into its protective jacket as shown.

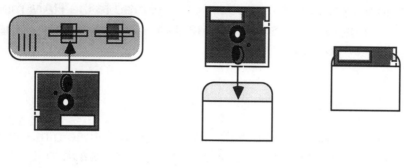

Software

The Major Categories of Software

Software represents the instructions (called <u>programs</u>) for the computer hardware to follow. You provide these programs as they are needed to accomplish the desired tasks. Once the computer receives these instructions, it follows them until further instructions are given. These programs generally fall into three categories: **operating systems**, **programming languages**, and **application programs**.

Operating Systems   Programming Languages   Application Programs

The **operating system software** directs the interaction of the hardware and software components. **Programming languages** allow you to develop general-purpose programs according to your specifications. **Application programs** are programs that perform general functions such as spreadsheets, word processing, or general ledger accounting.

The Disk Operating System (DOS)

The system software for the IBM PC microcomputer is often called <u>MS DOS</u>, or **DOS** for short. This is a software program written specifically for the IBM PC and contains many subprograms that control the interaction of the hardware and software components. When you start the computer, you will see a prompt as **A>**. This is DOS waiting for your request. At this point, you can load an application program such as the <u>VAC</u> program, or you can perform routine tasks such as listing the files stored on your floppy disk, formatting a blank disk for use in the IBM PC, or even erasing certain files on your disk to increase the usable space.

These routine tasks are performed by giving DOS specific commands. For example, to list the files on your disk, do the following.   At the **A>** prompt, type **DIR** and then press the **[Return]** key. This will display the files on the disk in Drive A. A few examples are shown.

Type	To do this
A> DIR [Return]	To display a directory of files on floppy disk in Drive A.
A> DIR B: [Return]	To display a directory of files on floppy disk in Drive B. Be sure to include the colon after B.
A> ERASE filename [Return]	To remove a specific file on Drive A.
A> ERASE B:filename [Return]	To remove a specific file on Drive B. Be sure to include the colon after B.

For other commands, please refer to the IBM DOS manual.

Appendix B - Problem Correlation

Computer Resource Guide - Fourth Edition

Problem Correlation for *Principles of Accounting*, Sixth Edition, by Hanson, Hamre, and Walgenbach, and published by Harcourt Brace Jovanovich, Inc.

PART ONE The Accounting Cycle, *Processing Business Transactions*

Chapter 2   THE DOUBLE-ENTRY ACCOUNTING SYSTEM
2-29 James Behm   2-29A Mary Aker
2-30 Morgan's Waterproofing Service   2-30A R. Ladd
2-32 Art Graphics   2-32A Mehl Dance Studio

Chapter 3   THE ACCOUNTING CYCLE
3-26 Ladd Roofing Service   3-26A Huang Karate School
3-27 Wellness Catering Service 3-27A Market-Probe
3-29 Dole Carpet Cleaners   3-29A The Wheel Place, Inc.

Chapter 4   THE ACCOUNTING CYCLE CONCLUDED
Mini Practice Set - Keith Howe, Tax Consultant
Mini Practice Set - Karen Fero, Attorney

Chapter 5   MERCHANDISING OPERATIONS
5-33 Wong Distributors   5-33A Lincoln Corporation

Chapter 6   ACCOUNTING SYSTEMS
6-27 Lincoln Distributors   6-27A Sterling Wholesalers
6-28 Rindt Distributors   6-28A Brown Distributors

PART TWO The Electronic Spreadsheet, *Analyzing Business Problems*

(The electronic file name is shown in parentheses.)

Chapter 7   INTERNAL CONTROL, CASH, SHORT-TERM INVESTMENTS
7-30 Sullivan Company **(BAN)**   7-30A Wallace Company

Chapter 8   TRADE ACCOUNTS AND NOTES
8-29 Schuler Company **(REC)**   8-29A Rinehart Company

Chapter 9   INVENTORIES
9-31 Venner Company **(LCM)**   9-31A Crane Company

Computer Resource Guide - Fourth Edition
Problem Correlation for *Financial Accounting*, Seventh Edition, by
Walgenbach and Hanson, and published by
Harcourt Brace Jovanovich, Inc.

PART ONE The Accounting Cycle, *Processing Business Transactions*

Chapter 2 THE DOUBLE-ENTRY ACCOUNTING SYSTEM
2-29 James Behm 2-29A Mary Aker
2-30 Morgan's Waterproofing Service 2-30A R. Ladd
2-32 Art Graphics 2-32A Mehl Dance Studio

Chapter 3 THE ACCOUNTING CYCLE
3-26 Ladd Roofing Service 3-26A Huang Karate School
3-27 Wellness Catering Service 3-27A Market-Probe
3-29 Dole Carpet Cleaners 3-29A The Wheel Place, Inc.

Chapter 4 THE ACCOUNTING CYCLE CONCLUDED
Mini Practice Set - Keith Howe, Tax Consultant
Mini Practice Set - Karen Fero, Attorney

Chapter 5 MERCHANDISING OPERATIONS
5-33 Wong Distributors 5-33A Lincoln Corporation

Chapter 6 ACCOUNTING SYSTEMS
6-27 Lincoln Distributors 6-27A Sterling Wholesalers
6-28 Rindt Distributors 6-28A Brown Distributors

PART TWO The Electronic Spreadsheet, *Analyzing Business Problems*
(The electronic file name is shown in parentheses.)

Chapter 7 INTERNAL CONTROL, CASH, SHORT-TERM INVESTMENTS
7-30 Sullivan Company **(BAN)** 7-30A Wallace Company

Chapter 8 TRADE ACCOUNTS AND NOTES
8-29 Schuler Company **(REC)** 8-29A Rinehart Company

Chapter 9 INVENTORIES
9-31 Venner Company **(LCM)** 9-31A Crane Company